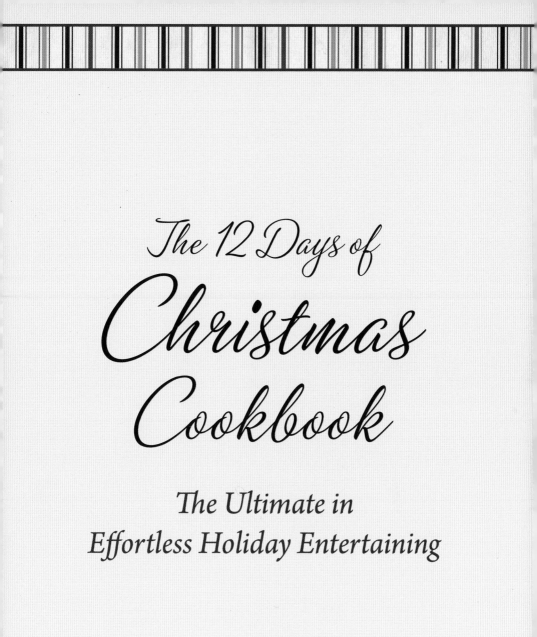

The 12 Days of
Christmas
Cookbook

The Ultimate in
Effortless Holiday Entertaining

BARBOUR
PUBLISHING

Published by Barbour Publishing, Inc., P.O. Box 719, Uhrichsville, Ohio 44683, www.barbourbooks.com

Our mission is to publish and distribute inspirational products offering exceptional value and biblical encouragement to the masses.

Member of the
Evangelical Christian
Publishers Association

Printed in China.

Contents

On the first day of Christmas my true love sent to me. . .

Delve into *The Twelve Days of Christmas Cookbook* where you're guaranteed to "unwrap" a delightful dish for every day of the Christmas season. With great ideas for beverages and breads, candies and cookies, main dishes and more—even a special section for kids in the kitchen—you'll find the perfect blend of recipes for your get-togethers. Happy holiday cooking!

Every good and perfect gift is from above, coming down from the Father of the heavenly lights.

James 1:17 NIV

Salads

Sides

Soups

Time was with most of us, when Christmas Day, encircling all our limited world like a magic ring, left nothing out for us to miss or seek; bound together all our home enjoyments, affections, and hopes; grouped everything and everyone round the Christmas fire, and made the little picture shining in our bright young eyes complete.

CHARLES DICKENS

On the first day of Christmas
my true love sent to me. . .

An Appetizer on a Platter

Appetizer, Anyone?

Appetizers only! . . . It's an economical, filling, and stress-free meal with lots of variety. Have each guest bring a favorite appetizer—finger foods are best. Your contributions as hostess are the beverages and a simple dessert, such as homemade cookies or bars that, like the appetizers, qualify as finger food. Encourage casual, comfortable dress when you extend the invitation.

This is a good time to bring out your fancy serving platters for presentation since some friends will arrive with their treats in Tupperware. (While you're at it, unbox your punch bowl—even the simplest entertaining needs a touch of flair! See the beverage section of this book for punch ideas.) Have your oven and microwave cleared and ready for those bringing hors d'oeuvres that need heating.

Remember to keep it casual when decorating. Forego your dining room table and opt for serving in the comfort of the family, hearth, or living room, perhaps near the Christmas tree. Arrange platters of appetizers on the coffee table along with plates and napkins for easy self-service. If you're using paper plates, be sure they're sturdy and display a cheerful holiday theme. Provide eating utensils only as needed—less is best! Low lamplight and candles around the room will relax and delight your guests, who are no doubt a bit harried this time of year. Encourage them to kick off their shoes and sit on the floor if they'd like.

Should conversation flag, ask guests to share their favorite Christmas memories. A discussion like this is a great way to help your guests become better acquainted. A good hostess makes sure that everyone gets a chance to talk, so keep the conversation moving around the room.

Send each guest home with a pretty Christmas recipe card on which you've printed your favorite appetizer recipe. As a reminder to keep the season focused on the reason for our celebrations, you may want to include the Bible passage that recounts the birth of Christ in a humble manger, the lowly expression to us of God's inestimable gift!

Effortless Entertaining Tips:

*Always make plenty of ice ahead of any gathering.

*Allow 30 minutes ahead of time for lighting the fire, setting out candles, putting
on music, and relaxing before your guests arrive.

{

*For unto us a child is born, unto us a son is given:
and the government shall be upon his shoulder:
and his name shall be called Wonderful, Counsellor, The mighty God,
The everlasting Father, The Prince of Peace.*

ISAIAH 9:6 KJV

}

Festive Nibbles

1 cup flour, plus extra for dusting
1 teaspoon mustard powder
Salt
½ cup butter, plus extra for greasing
3 ounces cheddar cheese, grated
Pinch cayenne pepper
2 tablespoons water
1 egg, beaten
Poppy seeds, sunflower seeds, or sesame seeds to decorate

Sift together flour, mustard powder, and salt. Cut butter into mixture until it resembles fine bread crumbs. Stir in cheese and cayenne and sprinkle water onto mixture. Add half the beaten egg, mix to a firm dough, and knead lightly until smooth. Roll out dough on lightly floured board. Using cookie cutters, cut out desired shapes and place on greased baking sheet, brushing tops with remaining egg. Sprinkle seeds over top to decorate and bake at 350 degrees for 10 minutes.

Bacon Crispies

¾ cup butter, softened
1½ cups flour
Salt and pepper to taste
½ cup cheddar cheese, grated
6 ounces finely chopped bacon

Heat oven to 325 degrees. Beat butter, flour, and salt and pepper until smooth. Add grated cheese and ⅔ of bacon and mix well. Drop by teaspoonfuls onto greased baking sheet, sprinkling with remaining bacon. Bake for 30 minutes or until lightly browned. Cool and store in airtight container. Makes 28 to 30 appetizers.

Parmesan Bread Sticks

    1 (1 pound) loaf French bread
    ¾ cup margarine or butter, melted
    ¼ cup grated Parmesan cheese

Preheat oven to 425 degrees. Cut bread loaf into 5 pieces, each about 4 inches long. Cut each piece lengthwise into 6 sticks. Brush sides with melted margarine or butter and sprinkle with Parmesan cheese. Place sticks on ungreased jelly-roll pan and bake about 8 minutes, or until golden. Makes about 30 bread sticks.

Barbecue Bites

2 cups barbecue sauce
2 cups grape jelly
2 pounds smoked sausage chunks or meatballs

Combine sauce and jelly. Place meat in slow cooker and pour sauce mixture over all. Set on medium heat and stir occasionally until meat is heated through.

Oat Snack Mix

½ cup butter
⅓ cup honey
¼ cup packed brown sugar
1 teaspoon cinnamon
½ teaspoon salt
3 cups oat cereal squares
1½ cups old-fashioned rolled oats
1 cup small pretzels
1 cup mixed nuts

In saucepan, combine butter, honey, brown sugar, cinnamon, and salt. Heat until butter melts, stirring until sugar dissolves. In large bowl, combine cereal, oats, pretzels, and nuts. Drizzle with butter mixture and mix well. Bake in 9x13-inch pan at 275 degrees for 45 minutes. Stir every 15 minutes. Yield: 6 cups.

Cheddar Stuffed Mushrooms

16 ounces fresh whole mushrooms, cleaned
2 tablespoons minced onion
¾ cup herb stuffing mix
½ cup sharp cheddar cheese, shredded
¼ cup butter, melted

Remove stems from mushrooms and set caps aside. Finely chop half the stems and discard the rest. In bowl, combine chopped mushrooms, onion, stuffing mix, cheese, and butter. Mix well. Spoon about a teaspoon of mixture into each mushroom cap. Place on greased cookie sheet. Bake at 350 degrees for 10 to 12 minutes. Serve warm.

Bacon Cheese Spread

1 pound round loaf bread
1 pound bacon, cooked crisp
8 ounces Colby and/or Monterey Jack cheese, shredded
1 cup Parmesan cheese, grated
1 cup mayonnaise
1 small onion, minced

Cut top off bread and hollow out center of loaf, leaving a 1-inch shell. (Reserve center bread pieces for dipping in the spread.) Mix bacon, cheeses, mayonnaise, and onion together. Spoon into bread bowl and top with bread lid. Place on baking sheet and bake at 350 degrees for 1 hour. Serve hot with bread, crackers, or tortilla chips.

Magic Meatball Sauce

1 (10 ounce) can condensed cream of chicken soup
1 (1 pound, 10 ounce) jar of spaghetti sauce, traditional recipe
1 (18 ounce) bottle spicy honey barbecue sauce

Warm soup on low heat or slowly in microwave, until lumps are gone and soup is smooth. Pour soup, spaghetti sauce, and barbecue sauce into slow cooker and add cooked, defrosted meatballs. Simmer until ready to eat.

Honey-Glazed Chicken Wings

3 pounds chicken wings
⅓ cup soy sauce
2 tablespoons oil
2 tablespoons chili sauce (or ketchup or barbecue sauce)
¼ cup honey
1 teaspoon salt
½ teaspoon ground ginger
¼ teaspoon garlic powder (or 1 clove garlic, minced)
¼ teaspoon cayenne pepper

Separate wings at joints and place in large bowl. In separate bowl, combine remaining ingredients. Pour mixture over chicken. Cover and refrigerate, turning chicken occasionally, at least one hour or overnight. Heat oven to 375 degrees. Drain chicken, reserving marinade. Place chicken on rack in foil-lined broiler pan. Bake 30 minutes. Brush chicken with reserved marinade. Turn chicken and bake

Chinese Chicken

1 can crushed pineapple
½ cup water
½ cup vinegar
½ cup brown sugar
Cornstarch
3 pounds chicken wings or drumettes

In bowl, combine pineapple, water, vinegar, and brown sugar. Thicken mixture with cornstarch. Marinate chicken for 2 hours. Bake at 350 degrees for 45 minutes on foil-lined baking sheet, turning once.

Microwave Mozza Mushrooms

12 medium fresh mushroom caps
4 slices bacon, cooked and crumbled
12 cubes mozzarella cheese
Grated Parmesan cheese

Place equal amount of crumbled bacon into each cap. Top with cheese cube. Place on microwave tray or glass dish. Microwave on high for about a minute or until cheese melts. Sprinkle with Parmesan cheese and serve.

Dried-Beef Ball

1 (8 ounce) package cream cheese, softened
¼ cup Parmesan cheese, grated
1 tablespoon prepared horseradish
1 cup dried beef, finely cut

Blend cheeses and horseradish; form mixture into ball. Cover and chill overnight. Roll ball in beef. Serve with assorted crackers.

Herb-and-Cheese-Filled Cherry Tomatoes

1 (4 ounce) package cream cheese, softened
½ teaspoon dried dill weed
1 teaspoon milk
15 to 16 cherry tomatoes

Combine cream cheese, dill, and milk and mix well. Remove top and seeds from each tomato. Drain tomatoes upside down on paper towel for a few minutes. Fill each tomato with cream cheese mixture. Chill or serve immediately.

Stuffed Bacon Rolls

¼ cup milk
1 egg, beaten
2 cups soft bread crumbs, about 3 slices
1 cup Granny Smith apple, finely chopped
1 tablespoon onion, finely chopped
1 tablespoon parsley, snipped
Salt and pepper to taste
10 or 11 slices bacon

In mixing bowl, combine milk and egg. Add bread crumbs, apple, onion, parsley, salt, and pepper; mix well. Cut each slice of bacon in half crosswise. Shape crumb mixture into balls, using one rounded tablespoon for each. Wrap each ball in bacon slice; secure with wooden pick. Place on wire rack set in 15x10-inch baking pan. Bake at 375 degrees for 30 minutes or until bacon is brown. Yield: 20

Water Chestnuts and Bacon

  1 to 2 pounds bacon strips, cut in half
  2 (8 ounce) cans whole water chestnuts
  ⅔ cup ketchup
  1 cup sugar

Wrap a piece of bacon around each chestnut and secure with a toothpick. Bake at 350 degrees for 30 minutes. Drain fat. Mix ketchup and sugar together and spoon over bacon chestnuts. Bake another 30 minutes.

Cheesy Mushroom Rounds

  2 (8 ounce) cans refrigerated crescent roll dough
  2 (8 ounce) packages cream cheese, softened
  3 (4 ounce) cans mushroom stems and pieces, drained and chopped
  1¼ teaspoons garlic powder
  ½ teaspoon Cajun seasoning
  1 egg
  1 tablespoon water
  2 tablespoons Parmesan cheese, grated

Unroll crescent roll dough into 2 long rectangles; seal seams and perforations to create one large piece. Combine cream cheese, mushrooms, garlic powder, and Cajun seasoning. Spread over dough to within 1 inch of edges. Roll up jelly-roll style. Seal edges and place seam side down on greased baking sheet. In bowl, beat together egg and water; brush over roll, and sprinkle roll with cheese. Bake at 375 degrees for 20 to 25 minutes or until golden brown. Cut into slices. Yield: 16 appetizers.

Broccoli Squares

2 (8 ounce) cans refrigerated crescent roll dough
2 (8 ounce) packages cream cheese, softened
1 cup mayonnaise
1 (1 ounce) package ranch dressing mix
1 head fresh broccoli, chopped into small pieces
3 Roma (plum) tomatoes, chopped
1 cup cheddar cheese, shredded

Preheat oven to 375 degrees. Arrange crescent roll dough in 4 rectangles on lightly greased baking sheet. Bake in preheated oven for 12 minutes or until golden brown. Remove from oven and allow to cool completely. In medium bowl, mix cream cheese, mayonnaise, and dry ranch dressing mix. Spread evenly over baked crescent roll rectangles. Sprinkle with broccoli and tomatoes. Top with cheddar cheese and serve.

Pita Bites

1 cup mayonnaise
1 onion, chopped
½ cup slivered almonds
½ pound cheddar cheese
6 slices cooked bacon, crumbled
1 bag pitas, halved and cut into triangles (or use mini-size pitas)

In bowl, combine all ingredients except pitas. Spread mixture on top of pita triangles. Bake at 400 degrees for 8 to 10 minutes.

Cheese Puffs

¾ cup butter or margarine
1 (3 ounce) package cream cheese
8 ounces sharp cheddar cheese
Tabasco sauce
Worcestershire sauce
Garlic salt
2 egg whites, beaten stiffly
1 white sandwich bread loaf (frozen)

Melt butter or margarine and cheeses together. Add sauces and garlic salt. Fold in beaten egg whites. Cut crusts off frozen loaf. Cut bread in cubes and dip each cube in cheese mixture. Place on greased cookie sheet and set in fridge overnight. Bake at 350 degrees for 15 minutes.

This is Christmas: not the tinsel , not the giving and receiving,
not even the carols, but the humble heart that receives anew
the wondrous gift, the Christ.

Frank McKibben

On the second day of Christmas
my true love sent to me:

Two Beverages a-Blending

After-Program Beverages and Snacks

After that Christmas program or choir cantata, your friends will be delighted when you invite them to your home for beverages and snacks. Don't make the mistake of waiting until the last minute. Plan ahead, and you'll please everyone who attends.

Begin by filling your punch bowl with a colorful, delicious punch. Make an ice ring of concentrated juices and fruit chunks; freeze it in a bundt pan or circular tube Jell-O mold. As the evening progresses, the ring will keep the punch cold and freshened as it melts. You only need to add fresh ginger ale once or twice as the punch is used up. If your punch is clear, have a bag of frozen cranberries ready to pull out of the freezer at the last minute. Drop these into the punch bowl or individual glasses of soda, sparkling water, or juice to serve as pretty, Christmassy ice cubes.

Slice up a beef summer sausage or cold ham and several types of cheeses; a beautiful cheese ball is always a hit. Slices of crusty French bread and a festive basket of assorted crackers make a perfect complement for your punch bowl. If you wish to offer a hot drink, fresh-brewed coffee or tea or a slow cooker simmering with wassail or apple cider will fill the air with wonderful seasonal aromas, while warming your guests. Eggnog or pumpkin nog goes a long way, because it is so rich, and adds to the holiday feel.

Let guests move around the table to serve themselves. If you don't keep Christmas china or dessert dishes for holiday use, buy clear plastic cups and plates available at your supermarket. Dollar stores are a good place to pick up inexpensive glass cups you'll need for hot drinks. This is a great investment, because they go with any china and can be used year-round. Splurge on pretty paper cocktail napkins.

For a centerpiece, buy an inexpensive clear glass bowl or wide cylindrical vase; fill half-way with cold water, cranberries, and floating candles. Arrange greenery around the base and turn the overhead lights down for ambience. Provide just enough light to allow guests to serve themselves.

Sing carols at the piano, or ask a musical guest to start everyone off a cappella.

There is something very relaxing and magical about a roomful of people sitting around in candlelight, harmonizing to a song. It can bring the true meaning of Christmas home to our hearts in a sweetly profound way, at a time of year when there is far too much stress.

For favors, go to a genuine candy store and buy real, old-fashioned candy canes—the big, fat ones that resemble barber poles. Tie each with a green or red velvet ribbon and display them in a tall glass vase as part of your décor, but make sure your guests take one as they leave.

Effortless Entertaining Tips:

*Ice rings take a long time to freeze, so get yours into the freezer at least two days before the party.

*Party dishes that are a plate and cup combo are regaining popularity. Look for them in resale shops—or your mother's attic!

*Citric acid in most punches will keep fruit from turning brown. If your punch has none, dip fruit chunks in a light water/lemon juice solution before freezing.

> This star drew nigh to the northwest.
> O'er Bethlehem it took its rest;
> And there it did both stop and stay,
> Right over the place where Jesus lay.
>
> TRADITIONAL ENGLISH CAROL

Frosty Lime Punch

2 (6 ounce) cans frozen limeade concentrate, thawed
3 cups cold water
2 (12 ounce) bottles lemon-lime carbonated beverage, chilled
1 cup lime sherbet

In large punch bowl, mix limeade concentrate, cold water, and carbonated beverage. Spoon scoops of sherbet into bowl and serve immediately. Yield: 15 (½ cup) servings.

Citrus Fizz

6 cups fresh orange or grapefruit juice, chilled
2 cups club soda

Mix juice and soda in glass pitcher. Stir briefly and serve immediately.

Sparkling Cranberry Punch

2 quarts cranberry juice cocktail, chilled
1 (6 ounce) can frozen lemonade concentrate, thawed
1 quart sparkling water

Mix cranberry juice cocktail and lemonade concentrate in large punch bowl. Just before serving, stir in chilled sparkling water. Yield: 25 (½ cup) servings.

Hot Cran-Apple Cider

2 quarts apple cider
1½ quarts cranberry juice cocktail
¼ cup packed brown sugar (optional)
4 (3 inch) sticks cinnamon
1½ teaspoons whole cloves
1 lemon, thinly sliced

Mix all ingredients together in large pot and bring to boil. Reduce heat
and simmer uncovered until flavors are blended, about 15 minutes. Remove
cinnamon, cloves, and lemon slices. Serve fresh lemon slices in each cup if
desired.

Spiced Tea

4 orange pekoe tea bags
Juice of 3 oranges and 3 lemons
4 teaspoons cinnamon
1½ teaspoons ground cloves
2 cups sugar
16 cups (1 gallon) water

Combine all ingredients in large saucepan. Simmer for 20 minutes, then remove tea bags. Serve immediately.

Hot Vanilla

4 cups milk
4 teaspoons honey
½ teaspoon vanilla extract
Ground cinnamon

In saucepan, heat milk until very hot, but do not boil. Remove from heat and stir in honey and vanilla. Divide between four mugs and sprinkle with cinnamon. Yield: 4 servings.

Creamy Dreamy Hot Chocolate

1 (14 ounce) can sweetened condensed milk
½ cup unsweetened cocoa powder
2 teaspoons vanilla extract
⅛ teaspoon salt
6½ cups hot water

Combine first four ingredients in large saucepan; mix well. Over medium heat, slowly stir in water. Cook until heated through, stirring frequently.

Orange Eggnog Punch

1 quart eggnog
1 (12 ounce) can frozen orange juice concentrate, thawed
1 (12 ounce) can ginger ale, chilled

In pitcher, mix eggnog and orange juice concentrate until well blended. Gradually pour in ginger ale and stir gently. Yield: 8 servings.

Fresh Berry Punch

    1 (12 ounce) bag fresh cranberries
    3 cups water
    1 envelope raspberry drink mix
    1 can frozen pineapple juice concentrate, thawed
    1 lemon, sliced
    1 (2 liter) bottle ginger ale

Puree 2 cups cranberries. Combine pureed cranberries, remaining whole cranberries, and water in large saucepan. Cook over high heat until cranberries begin to pop; remove from heat. Stir in remaining ingredients except ginger ale. Freeze mixture about 12 hours, stir, and refreeze. To serve: Puree slush in food processor, spoon into punch bowl, and mix in ginger ale.

Green Christmas Punch

2 envelopes lemon-lime drink mix
1½ cups sugar
2 quarts water
1 (20 ounce) can pineapple juice
1 (2 liter) bottle ginger ale
½ gallon lime sherbet
Maraschino cherries (optional)

Dissolve drink mix and sugar in 2 quarts water. Stir in pineapple juice. Chill. To serve, blend lemon-lime mixture with ginger ale in punch bowl. Place scoops of lime sherbet onto punch. If desired, place a maraschino cherry on each scoop of sherbet. Yield: 25 to 30 servings.

Fireside Mocha Mix

2 cups nondairy coffee creamer
1½ cups instant coffee mix
1½ cups hot cocoa mix
1½ cups sugar
1 teaspoon cinnamon
¼ teaspoon nutmeg

In large bowl, combine all ingredients. Store mixture in airtight container. To prepare one serving, stir 2 heaping tablespoons of mix into 1 cup boiling water. Yield: 40 prepared cups.

Creamy Orange Drink

6 cups orange juice, divided
1 teaspoon vanilla extract
1 (3.4 ounce) package instant vanilla pudding
1 envelope whipped topping mix

In large mixing bowl, combine half the orange juice with vanilla, pudding mix, and whipped topping mix. Beat until smooth; then mix in remaining juice. Chill thoroughly. Yield: 6 to 8 servings.

Holiday Punch

1 (3 ounce) box cherry-flavored gelatin
1 cup boiling water
1 (6 ounce) can frozen lemonade concentrate
3 cups cold water
1 quart cranberry juice
Ice cubes
1 (12 ounce) can ginger ale

Dissolve gelatin completely in boiling water. Stir in lemonade concentrate, cold water, and cranberry juice. Chill. Immediately before serving, pour mixture over ice cubes in large punch bowl. Stir in ginger ale. Yield: 25 to 30 servings.

Hot Christmas Punch

1½ quarts water
2 cups sugar
Juice of 3 oranges
Juice of 1 lemon
4 ounces red cinnamon candies
1 (20 ounce) can pineapple juice
2 quarts cranberry juice

In large saucepan, combine water, sugar, orange juice, lemon juice, and cinnamon candies. Bring to boil and stir until candies are dissolved. Add in pineapple juice and cranberry juice and cook over medium heat, stirring until punch is warmed through. Serve hot. Yield: 4 quarts.

New Year's Eve Punch

    1 (16 ounce) can fruit cocktail
    2 (6 ounce) cans frozen orange juice concentrate
    2 (6 ounce) cans frozen lemonade concentrate
    2 (6 ounce) cans frozen limeade concentrate
    2 (6 ounce) cans frozen pineapple concentrate
    1 pint raspberry sherbet

Pour fruit cocktail into ring mold and freeze overnight. Prepare frozen juices according to directions. Pour juices into 10-quart punch bowl and mix well. When ready to serve, float fruit cocktail ring in punch. Scoop sherbet into center of ring. Yield: 18 to 24 servings.

World's Best Cocoa

¼ cup cocoa
½ cup sugar
⅓ cup hot water
⅛ teaspoon salt
4 cups milk
¾ teaspoon vanilla extract

Mix cocoa, sugar, water, and salt in saucepan. Over medium heat, stir constantly until mixture boils. Continue to stir and boil for 1 minute. Add milk and heat through. (Do not boil.) Remove from heat and add vanilla; stir well. Pour into four mugs and serve immediately. Garnish with whipped cream and caramel

Pumpkin Nog

1 (16 ounce) can pumpkin puree
1 pint vanilla ice cream, softened
4 cups milk
1 teaspoon cinnamon
½ teaspoon nutmeg
¼ teaspoon ground ginger
Whipped topping

Combine in blender small portions of pumpkin, ice cream, milk, and spices; blend thoroughly. Pour into pitcher. Continue blending small amounts until all ingredients are combined in pitcher. Pour into mugs. Top with whipped cream and a sprinkle of cinnamon if desired. Yield: 10 servings.

Snowy Cinnamon Cocoa

4 cups milk
1 cup chocolate syrup
1 teaspoon cinnamon
Whipped topping
¼ cup semisweet chocolate chips

Place milk and chocolate syrup in microwave-safe bowl and stir. Microwave on high for 3 to 4 minutes or until hot. Stir in cinnamon. Pour into four large mugs and garnish with whipped topping and chocolate chips. Yield: 4 servings.

Somehow, not only for Christmas
But all the long year through,
The joy that you give to others
Is the joy that comes back to you.

JOHN GREENLEAF WHITTIER

*On the third day of Christmas
my true love sent to me:*

Three Breads a-Rising

Bread-Baking Festivities

There are plenty of enthusiastic bakers out there. Ask around and when you find someone, ask if he or she would be willing to demonstrate the process for a group in your home. These days, both men and women enjoy cooking, so this could be great fun for a mixed group.

You'll need to be able to stage the lesson using your kitchen island or breakfast table. Arrange a row or two of chairs in a semicircle for easy viewing. French bread or croissants are an ideal demonstration subject. Have several of the finished versions displayed. These can be served with the meal while the bread being made is left to rise.

Since your kitchen will be your entertaining area, decorate it to resemble a bakery. Have a variety of bakery breads stacked on a counter with a price card sticking out of the center. (Plan to use these right away, or freeze and use them as you have need during the holidays.) Use your cake stand with a glass cover to display a pie, cookies, muffins, or Danish on a doily with a toothpick price flag in each. Buy or borrow full-length white bakery aprons and chef hats for yourself and the demonstrator. You as hostess/host will be assistant to the "baker"—measuring, fetching, and keeping his/her workspace clear.

Encourage your guests to ask questions as the demonstration progresses. As host, you might want to read or recite certain bread-making facts while the demonstration is in progress: where to find French flour, early ovens, how grains are ground and milled, the types of pans needed, etc. Offer guests a variety of Christmas beverages and a light appetizer to be enjoyed during the demonstration. (Eggnog, punch, and tea are festive choices.)

Once the bread is left to rise, serve a meal in the dining room away from the hot kitchen. Offer a tossed salad and a hearty meat-based soup or stew that will complement the bread you've kept on hand to be served.

Your table service and décor should reflect a festive holiday theme. Since smaller bowls and salad plates are being used, your centerpiece theme can be a bit more extravagant: a crèche among boughs of greenery, apples and pears in a large wooden bowl, French loaves of varying shapes laid lengthwise down the center of the table. Just be sure your centerpiece is low enough to allow all your guests to see each other well! Add candle-light and low room light if your gathering takes place after dark.

As your guests are eating, present your demonstrator with a nice gift of appreciation and applause from the group.

Favors: Have each guest choose from a large Christmas basket filled with baking items (wooden spoons, measuring cups, oven mitts, a set of prep bowls, a kitchen towel, etc.). Tie each with a ribbon and Bible verse about Jesus being the bread of life: "And Jesus said unto them, I am the bread of life: he that cometh to me shall never hunger; and he that be-lieveth on me shall never thirst" (John 6:35 KJV).

Effortless Entertaining Tips:

* Bake your serving loaves well ahead of time but on the day of the party for maximum freshness.
* Advance preparation is key for the demonstration. Ask your demonstrator for a detailed shopping list and have all ingredients and prep items out or waiting in the refrigerator, ready to go.

{
Born thy people to deliver,
Born a child and yet a King,
Born to reign in us forever.
Now thy gracious kingdom bring.

CHARLES WESLEY
}

Sweet Potato Biscuits

4 cups flour
⅔ cup sugar
2 tablespoons baking powder
1½ teaspoons salt
2 cups sweet potatoes, warm, cooked, and mashed
½ cup oil or shortening
¼ cup milk

In large bowl, mix all ingredients together. Separate dough into pieces and roll into average-size biscuits. Bake on greased baking sheet at 475 degrees for 15 minutes. Yield: 36 rolls.

Holiday Muffins

½ cup vegetable oil
3 eggs
¼ cup brown sugar
2 teaspoons vanilla extract
1 carrot, peeled and grated
1 apple, peeled and grated
½ cup golden raisins
½ cup shredded coconut
1 cup flour
½ cup old-fashioned rolled oats
¼ cup wheat germ
½ cup chopped walnuts
1 teaspoon baking soda
1 teaspoon ground ginger
½ teaspoon baking powder
¼ teaspoon salt
Dash nutmeg

In mixing bowl, beat together oil, eggs, sugar, and vanilla until well blended. Add remaining ingredients. Mix on medium speed until all ingredients are blended. Do not overmix. Divide batter into greased muffin tins, filling to top of each cup. Bake about 20 minutes in a 375-degree oven.

Cheese Biscuits

    2 cups sifted flour
    3 teaspoons baking powder
    ½ teaspoon salt
    ¼ cup shortening
    ½ cup Swiss or cheddar cheese, grated
    ⅔ cup milk
    1 egg, slightly beaten
    2 to 3 tablespoons butter, melted

Sift dry ingredients together. Cut in shortening and cheese, mixing well. Add milk and egg, stirring quickly until soft dough is formed. Turn onto lightly floured surface and knead into smooth ball. Roll lightly to 2-inch thickness and cut into rounds with floured biscuit cutter. Bake on ungreased cookie sheet at 375 degrees for 12 to 15 minutes. Brush with melted butter immediately after removing from oven.

Apple Bread

2 medium apples, peeled and coarsely grated
2 tablespoons lemon juice
3 cups flour
1½ teaspoons baking soda
1 teaspoon salt
2½ teaspoons pumpkin pie spice
¾ cup shortening
1¼ cups packed brown sugar
3 eggs, room temperature
1½ teaspoons vanilla extract
¾ cup strong tea, room temperature
½ cup chopped nuts

In small bowl, mix grated apples with lemon juice and set aside. In separate bowl, combine flour, baking soda, salt, and spice; mix thoroughly and set aside. In another bowl, cream shortening and sugar. Add eggs, one at a time, beating well after each addition. Stir in apples and vanilla. Stir in flour mixture a little at a time, alternating with tea. Stir in nuts with last addition of dry ingredients. Pour into 2 greased 8x4-inch loaf pans. Bake in 350-degree oven for 1 hour or until bread tests done. Let stand 5 minutes; remove from pans, and cool on wire rack.

Nana's Banana Bread

1 cup sugar
⅓ cup butter or vegetable shortening
2 eggs, beaten
3 small overly ripened bananas, mashed
2½ cups flour, divided
1 teaspoon baking soda
6 tablespoons buttermilk
1 teaspoon vanilla extract
1 teaspoon lemon juice
Pinch salt
Chopped nuts (optional)

In mixing bowl, cream together sugar and butter. Add eggs and bananas. Add 1 cup flour. In separate bowl, stir baking soda into buttermilk and add to mixture. Add remaining flour, vanilla, lemon juice, and salt. Add chopped nuts, if desired. Grease and flour 1 large bread pan. Bake at 350 degrees for 45 minutes to 1 hour, testing with toothpick for doneness. Cool about 5 minutes, and remove from pan to rack.

Christmas Sweet Bread

1 cup butter
1 cup sugar
1 cup sorghum syrup
⅛ teaspoon baking soda
3 teaspoons baking powder
¼ teaspoon salt
3 cups flour
4 eggs, beaten

Over medium heat, melt butter in saucepan. Add sugar and syrup. Heat until lukewarm. In bowl, combine baking soda, baking powder, and salt with flour. Add to first mixture. Add well-beaten eggs and mix thoroughly. Pour into well-greased bread pan, and bake at 275 degrees 18 to 20 minutes or until done.

Pumpkin Bread

3 cups sugar
3½ cups flour
2 teaspoons baking soda
½ teaspoon salt
1 teaspoon cinnamon
1 teaspoon ground ginger
1 cup oil
4 eggs, beaten
⅔ cup water
1 (16 ounce) can pumpkin puree

Sift sugar, flour, baking soda, salt, and spices into large mixing bowl. Make a well in center of dry ingredients. Add oil, eggs, water, and pumpkin. Blend well; pour into 2 small greased loaf pans. Bake at 325 degrees for 1 hour and 10 minutes.

Christmas Pound Cake

1 pound butter
2 cups sugar
4 cups flour
12 eggs
2 teaspoons vanilla extract
1½ teaspoons lemon extract
½ teaspoon salt
½ teaspoon nutmeg
1 cup sour cream

In large bowl, cream butter and sugar. Slowly add flour and eggs. Add remaining ingredients and mix well. Bake for 1 hour at 325 degrees. Bake at 350 degrees for another 15 minutes. Cool completely. Wrap in foil, and tie with a festive ribbon.

Honey Wheat Bread

1½ cups water
1 cup cream-style cottage cheese
½ cup honey
¼ cup butter
6 cups flour, divided
1 egg
1 cup whole-wheat flour
2 tablespoons sugar
2 teaspoons salt
2 packages active dry yeast
Shortening
Extra butter

Heat water, cottage cheese, honey, and butter in medium saucepan over medium heat until very warm but not boiling. In large bowl, combine 2 leveled cups of flour with warm mixture. Add egg, whole-wheat flour, sugar, salt, and yeast. Beat for 2 minutes. By hand, stir in remaining flour to make stiff dough. Knead dough on well-floured surface until smooth and elastic (about 2 minutes). Place in greased bowl. Cover; let dough rise in warm place until light and doubled in size (45 to 60 minutes). Grease 2 loaf pans with shortening. Punch down dough; divide and shape into 2 loaves. Place in greased pans. Cover; let loaves rise in warm place until doubled in size. Heat oven to 350 degrees. Bake 40 to 50 minutes until loaves are deep golden brown and sound hollow when tapped. Immediately remove from pans. Brush with butter.

Mayonnaise Biscuits

1 cup whole milk
1 tablespoon sugar
2 tablespoons mayonnaise
2 cups self-rising flour

In large bowl, mix all ingredients. Spoon dough into greased muffin tins. Bake at 375 degrees for 15 minutes or until golden brown.

Gingerbread

2¼ cups flour
⅓ cup sugar
1 cup dark molasses
¾ cup hot water
½ cup shortening
1 egg
1 teaspoon baking soda
¾ teaspoon salt
1 teaspoon ground ginger
1¼ teaspoons cinnamon
Whipped topping

Combine all ingredients except whipped topping in large mixing bowl. Pour into greased 9-inch square pan. Bake at 325 degrees for 50 minutes. Cut into squares and serve warm with whipped topping. Optional: Garnish with crushed pepper-

Honey Apple Raisin Nut Bread

1 cup honey
½ cup shortening
 2 eggs, beaten
2 cups flour
¼ teaspoon salt
1 teaspoon baking soda
½ teaspoon cinnamon
⅛ teaspoon allspice
⅛ teaspoon ground cloves
1 cup applesauce
1 cup oatmeal
1 cup nuts, chopped
1 cup raisins

In large mixing bowl, blend honey and shortening. Mix in beaten eggs and beat until fluffy and light. In separate bowl, sift together flour, salt, baking soda, cinnamon, allspice, and cloves. Add dry mixture to honey mixture a little at a time, alternating with applesauce. Stir in oatmeal, nuts, and raisins. Pour into

Baking Powder Biscuits

2 cups flour
2 teaspoons baking powder
½ teaspoon salt
4 tablespoons butter, lard, or shortening
⅔ cup milk

Sift flour once; add baking powder and salt, and sift again. Cut in butter, lard, or shortening. Gradually add milk, stirring until soft dough is formed. Add an extra splash of milk if dough won't form. Turn out on lightly floured surface and gently knead for 30 seconds, just enough to shape. The key is to not work the dough too much. Roll to ½-inch thickness and cut with 2-inch floured biscuit cutter. Bake on ungreased sheet at 400 degrees for 12 to 15 minutes. Yield: 12 biscuits.

Hominy Bread

1 cup boiled hominy
1½ cups milk
¾ cup molasses
1 cup cornmeal
1 cup flour
1 tablespoon baking soda
1 teaspoon baking powder
1 teaspoon salt
1 egg, beaten
1 tablespoon shortening, melted

In bowl, mash hominy. Add milk and molasses to mashed hominy and beat together. In separate bowl, combine cornmeal, flour, baking soda, baking powder, and salt. Slowly add dry mixture to hominy. Add beaten egg and melted shortening. Place in greased loaf pan. Bake at 350 degrees for about 35 minutes.

Butter Pecan Bread

2¼ cups flour
2 teaspoons baking powder
½ teaspoon baking soda
½ teaspoon salt
¼ teaspoon cinnamon
¼ teaspoon nutmeg
1 cup light brown sugar
1 egg, beaten
1 cup buttermilk
2 tablespoons butter, melted
1 cup chopped pecans

Sift into bowl the flour, baking powder, baking soda, salt, and spices. Stir in brown sugar. Set aside. In separate bowl, combine egg, buttermilk, and butter. Add to flour mixture and blend well. Stir in chopped pecans. Turn batter into greased and floured 5×9-inch loaf pan. Bake at 350 degrees for 45 to 50 minutes or until wooden pick inserted in center comes out clean.

Pumpkin Cornbread

1½ cups cornmeal
½ cup whole-wheat flour
1 tablespoon baking powder
3 tablespoons sugar
1 teaspoon cinnamon
1 teaspoon salt
1 egg, beaten
3 tablespoons oil
¾ cup pumpkin puree
1½ cups milk

In large bowl, sift dry ingredients. In separate bowl, blend egg, oil, pumpkin, and milk. Combine with dry ingredients and mix lightly. Pour into greased 8x8-inch pan. Bake at 350 degrees for 30 to 35 minutes.

Pumpkin Muffins

2½ cups pumpkin puree
4 eggs
1 cup oil
1 cup water
4 cups flour
2¾ cups sugar
1¾ teaspoons baking soda
½ teaspoon baking powder
1 tablespoon cinnamon
1 tablespoon nutmeg
1 tablespoon ground cloves
1 teaspoon salt
1¼ cups raisins
¾ cup chopped walnuts

In large bowl, mix pumpkin, eggs, oil, and water. In another bowl, sift flour, sugar, baking soda, baking powder, cinnamon, nutmeg, cloves, and salt. Stir into pumpkin mixture. Add raisins and nuts. Line muffin tin cups with paper liners and fill each almost to top. Bake at 375 degrees for 15 minutes. Yield: 3½ dozen.

Christmas Morning Blueberry Biscuits

2¼ cups flour, divided
½ cup sugar
1 tablespoon baking powder
½ teaspoon fresh grated lemon peel
¾ teaspoon salt
¼ teaspoon baking soda
⅓ cup shortening
1 egg, lightly beaten

¾ cup buttermilk
¾ cup frozen blueberries,
  do not thaw
Topping:
3 tablespoons butter, melted
2 tablespoons sugar
¼ teaspoon cinnamon
Dash nutmeg

In large bowl, mix 2 cups flour with sugar, baking powder, lemon peel, salt, and baking soda. Cut in shortening until mixture is crumbly. In separate bowl, combine egg and buttermilk. Stir into flour mixture. Stir in frozen blueberries. Sprinkle remaining flour on flat surface. Flour fingers and gently knead dough just until it begins to hold together. Pat dough into ½-inch-thick rectangle. Cut with floured 2-inch round cutter. Place biscuits 2 inches apart on lightly greased baking sheet. Bake in center of preheated 400-degree oven for 12 to 15 minutes or until lightly browned. In bowl, combine all topping ingredients and brush over warm biscuits.

South African Overnight Bread

2 cakes compressed yeast or 2
  packages dry yeast
2½ quarts water
3 cups sugar
2 cups butter or margarine

1 (14 ounce) can sweetened
  condensed milk
2 teaspoons salt
10 cups flour
4 eggs, well beaten

In saucepan, slowly heat yeast, water, sugar, butter or margarine, and condensed milk. In large bowl, combine salt and flour; add eggs and warm milk mixture to flour and knead well. Cover and let rise in warm place overnight. Form into balls and place on baking sheets. Cover and let rise again. Bake at 375 degrees for 45 minutes.

Cinnamon Sticky Buns

2 loaves frozen bread dough, thawed
1 cup pecans, chopped
1 cup butter
1 cup brown sugar
1 (5 ounce) package instant vanilla pudding mix
2 teaspoons cinnamon
2 tablespoons milk

Let bread dough rise. Grease large cake pan and cover bottom with chopped pecans. Roll pieces of dough into 1-inch balls and place on top of nuts. Combine butter, brown sugar, pudding, cinnamon, and milk. Spread mixture over dough balls. Cover with plastic wrap. Let rolls rise in refrigerator overnight. Bake at 350

*What is Christmas? . . . It is a fervent wish that every cup may
overflow with blessings rich and eternal,
and that every path may lead to peace.*

Agnes M. Pharo

On the fourth day of Christmas
my true love sent to me:

Four Breakfast
Dishes a-Baking

Breakfast or Brunch

A breakfast event can be a fairly economical and simple affair. Whether you're cooking for a house full of guests or a small group of friends, these recipes will fill the bill nicely. Breakfast is a great time to try a wider variety of foods and get everyone into the action. The close quarters and a bit of chaos are all part of the fun! The host and hostess decide the menu ahead of time and do all the shopping. It's a good idea to make a list of each food that will be prepared. Think through who will best be in charge of it. Think, too, about the counter space and equipment each area will require for preparation.

Pair up kids with an adult to do simple jobs like helping with the table set-up and placing favors at each place. Put couples to work cutting up fruit, pouring drinks and making coffee, flipping pancakes or scrambling eggs; appoint someone to clean up "as you go" style. If you opt for a casserole, it will need to be ready the night before and put into the oven to bake first thing in the morning. Coffee cake or bread should be made the day before, as well. (Biscuits must be made just before eating, however, so make sure there is room in the oven for them.)

Give your busy breakfast restaurant a name (Sunshine Bakery, Early Bird Café). Make a sign to that effect and hang it on the refrigerator or tape it to the microwave door. A tent card with the name on both sides can be placed on the table, too.

Give your table a café or diner feel by decorating with a metal napkin holder, ketchup and mustard, salt and pepper, a bowl of single-servings of half & half, and a stack of individual serving jams and jellies. These can be found at restaurant supply stores, but a local breakfast eatery will most likely loan or sell you any of these items for your décor theme. Make paper place mats with your restaurant name on them, "Welcome to the Greasy Spoon," for example. Choose lively Christmas music (from the fifties, if possible).

Reserve a space on the place mat for a game called "Ham it up." Have spaces numbered 1–10 beneath the game title. As they eat, ask diners to list 10 breakfast food ingredients they think no one else will name. When everyone is finished, go around and have each person read his list. Any items found on any other lists get crossed out on all lists. The winner is the player who has managed to come up with the most items that are unique to his list. Genuine breakfast ingredient judgment calls are made by the host!

Favors could be small jars of jam, miniature loaves of breakfast bread, or cinnamon rolls. Wrap breads and rolls individually in Christmas plastic wrap for a festive presentation, and tie curly ribbon around the necks of the jam jars.

Effortless Entertaining Tips:

*Put juices in the refrigerator the night before, and have big pitchers of milk and
   ice water available.

*Think ahead about the use of the stove top; try to stagger preparation of eggs or
   pancakes to allow room for both.

*Set your oven temperature just warm enough to keep food hot as it is prepared.

*Always prepare breakfast meats a day in advance. They take too much time
   and space to cook with the other meal items. Store the cooked meat in the
   refrigerator and then microwave a batch at a time just enough to reheat
   and crisp it up, only about a minute in most cases.

*Use a pump-pot or thermos carafe for make-ahead hot drinks. They go fast!

{ *When they saw the star, they were overjoyed. . . . They saw the
child with his mother Mary, and they bowed down and worshiped him.
Then they opened their treasures and presented him with gifts* }

Creamed Eggs and Biscuits

6 tablespoons butter
6 tablespoons flour
1½ teaspoons salt
Dash black pepper
3 cups milk
6 hard-boiled eggs, chopped
Ham or bacon, chopped

In saucepan, melt butter on low heat; stir in flour, salt, and pepper until well blended. Slowly add milk and stir constantly. Cook until smooth. Add eggs and ham. Serve over toast or biscuits. Yield: 6 servings.

Cornmeal Mush

2¾ cups water
1 cup yellow cornmeal
1 cup cold water
1 teaspoon salt
1 teaspoon sugar

In large saucepan, bring water to boil. In bowl, combine remaining ingredients and add to boiling water, stirring constantly. Cook over medium heat until mixture is thick, stirring frequently. Cover pot and continue cooking 10 to 15 minutes over low heat. At this point, you may serve the hot mush with topping of fried sausage and onions and a bit of butter, if desired. Otherwise, pour hot mush into lightly greased loaf pan and refrigerate for several hours. Turn out of pan and cut into ½-inch slices. Deep fry in oil until golden brown. Serve with butter and syrup.

Deluxe Grits

 4 cups water
 1 cup old-fashioned grits
 ¼ cup butter
 1 teaspoon salt
 2 cups cheddar cheese, shredded
 6 to 8 slices bacon
 4 eggs
 1 cup milk

In 3-quart saucepan, bring water, grits, butter, and salt to boil. Reduce heat to simmer for 10 minutes. Stir in cheese until melted. Allow grits to continue to simmer while frying bacon in skillet until crisp. In small bowl, beat eggs with milk. Remove grits from heat and combine with eggs. Pour mixture into well-greased 9x13-inch pan. Bake at 350 degrees for 20 to 30 minutes. Crumble bacon on top and sprinkle with more shredded cheese to taste. Yield: 8 servings.

Apple Pancakes

2 eggs
2 cups flour, sifted
1 cup milk
1 cup applesauce
1 teaspoon salt
2 tablespoons baking powder
4 tablespoons butter, melted

In large bowl, combine all ingredients, mixing until smooth. Drop scoops of mixture on hot griddle or skillet, and fry pancakes until golden brown. Serve warm with syrup. Yield: about 16 pancakes.

Baked Oatmeal

1 cup sugar
½ cup oil
2 eggs
2 teaspoons baking powder
3 cups quick-cooking oatmeal
1 cup milk
¾ cup coconut
¼ cup pecans, chopped

In large bowl, mix all ingredients and pour into lightly greased 8x8-inch baking pan. Bake at 350 degrees for 30 minutes.

Breakfast Casserole

6 to 8 slices bread, torn into small pieces
1 pound sausage, cooked and crumbled
1 cup cheddar cheese, shredded
6 to 8 eggs
2 cups milk
1 teaspoon mustard
¼ teaspoon salt

Grease 9x13-inch pan and place bread pieces in bottom. Sprinkle sausage and cheese over bread. In large bowl, beat eggs and milk until fluffy, and add mustard and salt. Pour over bread, sausage, and cheese. Can be refrigerated overnight. Bake at 350 degrees for 45 minutes.

Swedish Oven Pancakes

½ cup butter
4 eggs
1 teaspoon salt
4 cups milk
2 cups flour

Heat oven to 400 degrees and place butter in 9x13-inch pan to melt in oven. In bowl, combine all other ingredients and pour into hot buttered pan. Bake for 35 to 40 minutes or until set. Serve with syrup.

Cinnamon Coffee Cake

1½ cups flour
½ cup granulated sugar
2½ teaspoons baking powder
½ teaspoon salt
¼ cup oil
1 egg
¾ cup milk
½ cup brown sugar
2 tablespoons flour
2 tablespoons oil
2 teaspoons cinnamon

In bowl, sift together flour, sugar, baking powder, and salt. In separate bowl, combine ¼ cup oil, egg, and milk; blend into dry mixture for batter. In another bowl, combine brown sugar, flour, 2 tablespoons oil, and cinnamon. Pour half of batter in greased 8x8-inch pan. Top with half of cinnamon-sugar mixture. Add remaining batter and top with remaining cinnamon-sugar mixture. Bake at 350 degrees for 20 to 25 minutes.

Holiday Breakfast Grits

    1 quart eggnog
    5 tablespoons butter
    1 cup uncooked grits
    1 teaspoon salt
    2 cups fresh blueberries

In large saucepan, warm eggnog and butter over low heat. Add grits and salt slowly while stirring. Keep stirring for about 25 minutes or until bubbly. Add blueberries and cook for 5 more minutes.

Grandma's Sausage Gravy and Country Biscuits

Gravy:
1 pound seasoned pork sausage
2 tablespoons flour
2 cups milk
Salt and pepper to taste

Brown sausage; drain, reserving 2 tablespoons grease; set aside. Stir in flour and gradually add milk. Stir over medium heat until gravy thickens. Add salt and pepper. Serve over split Country Biscuits (recipe follows).

Country Biscuits:
2 cups flour
½ teaspoon salt
3 teaspoons baking powder
⅓ cup plus 2 tablespoons shortening, divided
1 cup milk

Sift dry ingredients into mixing bowl. Using pastry blender or fork, cut in ⅓ cup shortening until mixture resembles coarse crumbs. Add milk and mix until dough forms soft ball. Turn out on lightly floured surface; knead gently for 1 minute. Roll to ½-inch thickness and cut with 2-inch round cutter. Melt 2 tablespoons shortening and pour into baking pan. Place biscuits in pan, turning so each side gets greased in melted shortening. Bake at 450 degrees until golden brown, approximately 15 minutes. Yield: 12 to 15 biscuits.

Blueberry Coffee Cake

Cake:
¾ cup sugar
¼ cup butter
1 egg
½ cup milk
2 cups flour
2 teaspoons baking powder
½ teaspoon salt
2 cups blueberries, partially
   frozen

Topping:
1 cup sugar
⅔ cup flour
½ cup butter
1 teaspoon cinnamon

In large bowl, mix cake ingredients. Pour batter into greased and floured 9x13-inch pan; set aside. In separate bowl, mix topping ingredients and sprinkle topping over cake batter. Can also be made into muffins. Bake 35 to 40 minutes at 350 degrees.

Cinnamon Toast

½ cup brown sugar
½ teaspoon cinnamon
1 tablespoon milk
½ stick butter (4 tablespoons), melted
10 to 12 slices bread

Mix together brown sugar, cinnamon, and milk; add melted butter. Place bread slices on baking sheet; spoon and spread cinnamon mixture over each slice. Place on middle rack of oven and broil for 2 to 3 minutes.

Coffee Break Cake

Cake:
½ cup butter or margarine
1 cup granulated sugar
1 tablespoon brown sugar
1 egg, unbeaten
2 cups flour
½ teaspoon salt
2 teaspoons baking powder
¾ cup milk
1 teaspoon vanilla
¼ teaspoon pure almond
    extract

Topping:
Before baking, mix
½ cup sugar
2 tablespoons melted butter
1 ½ teaspoons cinnamon

In large bowl, combine all cake ingredients in order given. Pour batter into greased 7x11-inch pan; set aside. Mix topping ingredients until crumbly; sprinkle over batter. Bake at 400 degrees for 25 minutes.

Glazed Breakfast Fruit

    4 pears, quartered
    4 peaches, quartered
    6 apricots, quartered
    1 cup brown sugar or to taste
    ½ stick butter

Place quartered fruits in shallow baking dish. Sprinkle with brown sugar; dot with butter. Bake at 450 degrees for 15 to 20 minutes until bubbly. (May use canned fruit.)

Cinnamon-Topped Oatmeal Muffins

1 cup flour
¼ cup sugar
3 teaspoons baking powder
½ teaspoon salt
1 cup quick-cooking oats
½ cup raisins
3 tablespoons oil
1 egg, beaten
1 cup milk

Topping:
2 tablespoons sugar
2 teaspoons flour
1 teaspoon cinnamon
1 teaspoon melted butter
1 cup old-fashioned oats

Preheat oven to 425 degrees. Sift together into mixing bowl, flour, sugar, baking powder, and salt. Stir in oats, raisins, oil, egg, and milk. Stir only until dry ingredients are moistened. Fill greased muffin cups ⅔ full; set aside. In small bowl, combine all topping ingredients and sprinkle topping over each muffin. Bake 15 minutes.

Country Breakfast

     9 eggs, lightly beaten
     ¾ cup milk
     ¼ cup margarine, melted
     1 pound sausage, browned and drained
     4½ cups frozen hash browns
     8 ounces cheddar cheese, grated

Preheat oven to 350 degrees. In bowl, with wire whisk, mix eggs, milk, and margarine. Layer sausage on bottom of greased 9x13-inch pan. Add hash browns on top of sausage, and pour egg mixture over layers. Sprinkle cheese over top. Bake 1 hour.

Buttermilk Pancakes

     2 cups sifted flour
     1 teaspoon soda
     1 teaspoon salt
     2 tablespoons sugar
     2 eggs, beaten
     2 cups buttermilk
     2 tablespoons oil
     1 teaspoon vanilla extract

In large bowl, combine dry ingredients. Add remaining ingredients and stir just until moistened. Pour scoops of batter onto hot griddle or skillet. Fry pancakes until golden brown; serve warm with syrup.

Caramel Apple Grits

1 cup heavy cream
2 cups whole milk
1 teaspoon cinnamon
1 teaspoon salt
½ teaspoon vanilla extract
3 tablespoons brown sugar
¾ cup uncooked grits
3 Granny Smith apples, peeled and sliced just before serving
Butter and brown sugar
¼ cup caramel syrup

Lightly oil six 1-cup ramekins (small baking dishes) and set aside. In heavy saucepan, stir together cream, milk, cinnamon, salt, vanilla, and 3 tablespoons brown sugar. Bring to boil and stir in grits. Cook over low heat, stirring frequently for 25 minutes or until thick and creamy. Spoon into ramekins, smoothing tops with spoon. Cover with plastic wrap and refrigerate overnight. Before serving, sauté apples with butter and brown sugar until tender. Warm grits in microwave until heated through. Warm caramel syrup for 45 seconds. Unmold warm grits onto plates and top with syrup and apples. Yield: 6 servings.

Bacon Gravy

2 to 4 slices bacon, cut into small pieces
⅓ cup flour
½ teaspoon salt
⅛ teaspoon black pepper
1 teaspoon sugar
3 cups milk

Fry bacon pieces over medium heat until crisp. Stir in flour until grease is absorbed. Season with salt, pepper, and sugar. Slowly whisk in milk, stirring until it reaches a boil. Boil for 5 minutes until thick. Serve over biscuits, toast, or potatoes.

I heard the bells on Christmas Day
Their old familiar carols play,
And wild and sweet the words repeat
Of peace on earth, good will to men!

HENRY WADSWORTH LONGFELLOW

On the fifth day of Christmas
my true love sent to me:

Five Candies

Old-Fashioned Christmas Tea

Candy making tends to be a tricky and intimidating business. In the past, only the most intrepid cooks would attempt it. But with modern equipment and simpler techniques, most of us can now step into the arena with confidence. Invite friends for an old-fashioned Christmas Tea. Send out invitations on cards with warm Christmas themes. (If you must e-vite, use tea party or Christmas artwork to dress it up.) Assign each guest one of the wonderful recipes in this section; you want to have a nice variety of candies, but trying to prepare them all yourself is a nearly impossible undertaking at this hectic time of year. Be sure to include the recipe in the invitation. Ask your guests to bring the finished product on a pretty Christmas plate or glass pedestal cake holder for presentation.

A tea is usually held mid-afternoon with very light refreshments. (Note: Tea is typically an all-ladies event, with a lot of breakable fine china involved, so suggest that guests leave the kids home with Dad.) Serve crustless finger sandwiches and a tray of fresh vegetables along with the candies. Place plates of food and treats all along the table and invite guests to serve themselves. Learn how to brew a pot of tea. Follow instructions on the tea boxes for guidance and practice ahead as brew times vary. Be sure to have a caffeine-free or herbal variety available. No tea bags allowed!

This is an old-fashioned tea, and as hostess, your job will be, if you don't own them, to borrow a pretty selection of teapots, cream and sugar vessels, teaspoons and small plates. An eclectic presentation of teacups and saucers is beautiful and fun, but few of us keep this kind of collection. Borrow pretty sets from friends. The overriding quality of this kind of tea party is elegance, so make sure you have a crisp, white linen tablecloth and cloth tea napkins. You can make your own napkins out of a yard of good fabric cut into small squares and hemmed with lace. For your centerpiece, fresh-cut flowers are a must, adding elegance to the gathering. They need not be expensive, but keep them low and choose rich Christmas colors. If you have room, decorate with clear glass apothecary jars filled with ribbon candy, candy canes, or a colorful mix of other old-fashioned Christmas candy. Have soft, relaxing Christmas instrumentals playing for ambience.

If you wish, and if time allows, ask one of your guests who has agreed in advance, to demonstrate a simple take on an intimidating candy recipe, such as fudge. This activity will of course be taking place in the kitchen, so ask guests to stand and watch or, if there's room, bring in their chairs. This activity is a fun conclusion to tea and can be a big encouragement to candy making novices. Keep the demonstration to 20 or 30 minutes.

Effortless Entertaining Tips:

*Be sure to return all borrowed china, cleaned and well-packed, within a day or two of your event.

*Serve real cream, sugar, and sliced lemons with tea. Old-fashioned sugar cubes are fun.

*Have all ingredients and equipment for a demonstration on hand.

*Let each guest take home a selection of candies as a favor. Have Christmas zipper storage bags available if needed.

> Good news from heaven the angels bring,
> Glad tidings to the earth they sing:
> To us this day a child is given,
> To crown us with the joy of heaven.
>
> MARTIN LUTHER

Coconut Macaroons

2½ cups sugar
2⅓ cups (8 ounces) shredded, fresh, unsweetened coconut
1 cup egg whites (whites of about 6 extra-large eggs)
1 teaspoon vanilla extract
⅓ cup plus 2 tablespoons flour
Baker's parchment paper

Preheat oven to 350 degrees. Butter cookie sheet and cover with parchment paper. Mix sugar, coconut, and egg whites in top of double boiler and stir over boiling water until mixture reaches 170 degrees on candy thermometer. Remove from heat, and stir in vanilla and flour. Using pastry bag with no nozzle, pipe macaroons about 1½ inches in diameter onto parchment paper. If you have no pastry bag, two teaspoons may be used to scoop batter instead. Bake for 15 minutes or until macaroons begin to turn pale gold. Remove from parchment and cool on rack. Macaroons will keep for several weeks in airtight container kept in cool place.

Chocolate Truffles

6 ounces semisweet chocolate baking squares
3 tablespoons unsalted butter
2 tablespoons powdered sugar
3 egg yolks
1 tablespoon rum flavoring
½ cup finely grated semisweet chocolate

Melt chocolate squares in top of double boiler over boiling water. Blend in butter and sugar, and stir until sugar dissolves. Remove from heat and add egg yolks, one at a time, beating well after each addition. Stir in rum flavoring. Place mixture in bowl covered with waxed paper overnight, but do not chill. Shape into 1-inch-diameter balls and roll in grated chocolate. Set truffles aside for a few days before eating. Yield: 2 dozen.

Easy Chocolate Fudge

    1 cup granulated sugar
    ¼ cup cocoa
    ⅓ cup milk
    ¼ cup margarine or butter
    1 tablespoon light corn syrup
    1 teaspoon vanilla extract
    2 to 2¼ cups powdered sugar

Combine granulated sugar and cocoa in 2-quart saucepan. Stir in milk, margarine or butter, and corn syrup. Bring to boil over medium heat, stirring frequently. Boil and stir 1 minute. Remove from heat and allow to cool without stirring until bottom of pan is lukewarm (about 45 minutes). Stir in vanilla. Mix in powdered sugar until very stiff. Press in buttered loaf pan measuring 9x5x3 inches. Chill until firm and cut into 1-inch squares. Yield: 32 candies.

Choco-Butterscotch Crisps

1 cup butterscotch chips
½ cup peanut butter
4 cups crisp rice cereal
1 cup chocolate chips
2 tablespoons butter
1 tablespoon water
½ cup powdered sugar

In large saucepan, melt butterscotch chips and peanut butter over very low heat, stirring occasionally. Add cereal and mix well. Press half of mixture into 8x8-inch square pan and chill. Melt chocolate chips, butter, and water in top of double boiler and add powdered sugar. Spread over chilled mixture and press in remainder of cereal mixture. Cut and chill.

Popcorn Balls

½ cup sugar
½ cup light corn syrup
½ cup margarine or butter
½ teaspoon salt
2 to 3 drops food coloring (optional)
8 cups popped corn, unpopped hulls removed

Simmer sugar, corn syrup, margarine or butter, salt, and food coloring in 4-quart Dutch oven over medium-high heat, stirring constantly. Add popped corn and cook about 3 minutes, stirring until popcorn is well coated. Remove from heat and cool slightly. After dipping hands into cold water, shape mixture into 2½- inch balls. Place balls on waxed paper and when cooled, wrap individually in plastic wrap. Yield: 8 to 9 popcorn balls.

Peanut Butter Bonbons

1½ cups powdered sugar
1 cup graham cracker crumbs (about 12 squares)
½ cup margarine or butter
½ cup peanut butter
1 (6 ounce) package semisweet chocolate chips
1 tablespoon shortening

In bowl, combine powdered sugar and cracker crumbs. In saucepan, melt margarine or butter and peanut butter over low heat and stir into crumb mixture. Shape into 1-inch balls. In double boiler, melt chocolate chips with 1 tablespoon shortening, and dip balls into chocolate with tongs until coated. Place on waxed paper and chill until firm. Optional: Drizzle melted chocolate on top of firmed bonbons to create decorative texture. Yield: 3 dozen candies.

Butterscotch Delights

1½ cups mini marshmallows
1 cup pecan pieces
2 cups (12 ounces) butterscotch chips
½ cup sweetened condensed milk

Butter 9x13-inch pan. Spread marshmallows and pecan pieces evenly on bottom of pan. In saucepan, combine butterscotch chips and condensed milk. Stir constantly over low heat until chips are melted. Pour mixture over marshmallows and nuts in pan. Use spatula to spread mixture evenly. Let stand at room temperature until set. Cut into squares. Store in tightly covered container in refrigerator.

Chocolate Caramels

2½ tablespoons butter
2 cups molasses
1 cup brown sugar
½ cup whole milk
1 square semisweet baking chocolate, chopped
1 teaspoon vanilla extract

In saucepan, combine butter, molasses, brown sugar, and milk. Cook over low heat until butter is melted and mixture is blended well. Add chocolate. Stirring constantly, heat until chocolate is completely melted. Boil mixture until candy thermometer reads 248 degrees. Remove from heat. Add vanilla and stir well. Pour into buttered 8x8-inch pan. Cool. Cut into squares.

Haystacks

1½ cups peanut butter
3 cups butterscotch chips
1 cup pretzel sticks

In saucepan, melt peanut butter and butterscotch chips over low heat. Remove from heat. Pour over pretzel sticks set in bowl. Stir to coat. Drop by teaspoonfuls onto waxed paper. Cool.

Toffee

1 cup pecan pieces
1½ cups brown sugar
1 cup butter
1 teaspoon vanilla extract

Spread pecan pieces on buttered baking sheet. Set aside. In saucepan, boil brown sugar and butter until candy thermometer reads 290 degrees. Remove from heat and stir in vanilla. Pour over pecan pieces. Let cool completely. Break into pieces.

Caramel Popcorn

¼ cup butter
½ cup light corn syrup
1 cup brown sugar
⅔ cup sweetened condensed milk
1 teaspoon vanilla extract
5 cups popped corn, unpopped hulls removed

In large saucepan, combine butter, corn syrup, and brown sugar. Bring to boil. Add condensed milk and return to boil, stirring constantly. Remove from heat and stir in vanilla. In large bowl, combine popped corn and caramel mixture, stirring well to coat. Spread popcorn on waxed paper to set. When cooled, break apart large pieces and store in an airtight container.

Christmas Crunchies

1 (6 ounce) package butterscotch chips
½ cup crunchy peanut butter
5 cups crisp rice cereal

In saucepan, stir butterscotch chips and peanut butter over low heat until butterscotch chips melt. Pour mixture over cereal in large bowl. Stir gently until cereal is completely coated. Drop by teaspoonfuls onto waxed paper. Chill in refrigerator for at least 2 hours.

Caramel Nut Cups

2 cups semisweet chocolate chips
1 tablespoon butter
¾ cup pecan pieces
¾ cup caramel ice-cream topping

In small saucepan over low heat, melt chocolate chips with butter, stirring constantly. Spoon about ½ tablespoon mixture into 36 small foil cups. With back of spoon, spread chocolate up sides of each cup, forming hollow center. Refrigerate until firm. Mix pecan pieces with caramel ice-cream topping. Spoon mixture into chocolate cups. Refrigerate.

Turtles

1 cup cashews
36 caramels, unwrapped
½ cup milk chocolate chips, melted

Preheat oven to 325 degrees. Arrange nuts in clusters on a greased cookie sheet.
Place 1 caramel in middle of each cluster. Heat in oven until caramels soften,
about 4 to 8 minutes. Remove from oven. Flatten caramels slightly. Cool briefly,
then remove from pan to waxed paper. Swirl melted chocolate on top of each
cluster.

Peanut Nougat

   2 cups sugar
   2 cups chopped peanuts

In 10-inch skillet, melt sugar to a syrup over low heat, stirring constantly. As soon as sugar is syrupy, add peanuts and stir quickly to coat. Remove from heat. Pour at once into warmed and buttered 8x8-inch pan. Allow to cool. Cut into squares.

Bull's Eyes

½ cup crunchy peanut butter
6 tablespoons butter, softened
1 tablespoon light corn syrup
1 teaspoon vanilla extract
2 cups powdered sugar
1 cup graham cracker crumbs
¾ cup semisweet chocolate chips
2 tablespoons shortening

In large bowl, beat peanut butter, butter, corn syrup, and vanilla on medium speed until smooth. Beat in sugar and cracker crumbs on low speed until well mixed. Mixture will look dry. Shape into 1-inch balls. In microwavable bowl, melt chocolate chips and shortening on high for 1 minute. Stir. Melt on high for 30 seconds more or until completely melted. With dipping spoon, dip peanut butter balls in chocolate mixture. Place on baking sheet lined with waxed paper. Let chocolate set completely before storing balls in tightly covered container.

Crispy Cereal Chocolate Drops

2 cups (12 ounces) butterscotch chips
1 cup (6 ounces) semisweet chocolate chips
½ cup salted peanuts
4 cups crisp cereal (almost any cereal will work)

Melt butterscotch chips and chocolate chips over very low heat, stirring constantly until smooth. Remove from heat. Add peanuts and cereal. Stir carefully until well coated. Drop by teaspoonfuls onto waxed paper. Chill until firm. Yield: 8 dozen.

Christmas Pralines

1 cup brown sugar
½ cup granulated sugar
½ cup heavy cream
¼ cup light corn syrup
1 tablespoon butter
1 teaspoon vanilla extract
1½ cups pecan pieces

In saucepan, combine sugars, cream, and corn syrup. Stirring frequently, bring to boil over medium heat. Reduce heat to low. Cook until candy thermometer reaches 238 degrees. Remove from heat. Add butter and vanilla. Beat with wooden spoon for 1 to 2 minutes or until mixture begins to thicken. Stir in pecan pieces. Stir to coat nuts well. Drop mixture by tablespoons onto baking sheet lined with waxed paper. Allow to cool. Store in tightly covered container with waxed paper between layers of pralines.

Banana Clusters

1 (12 ounce) package semisweet chocolate chips
⅓ cup peanut butter
1 cup unsalted peanuts
1 cup banana chips

Put chocolate chips and peanut butter in large microwavable bowl. Microwave on high for 2 minutes, stirring after 1 minute, or until chips are melted and mixture is smooth. Fold in peanuts and banana chips. Drop by rounded teaspoonfuls onto waxed paper that has been sprayed with butter-flavored nonstick cooking spray. Refrigerate until firm. Store in tightly covered container in refrigerator.

Cashew Brittle

2 cups (12 ounces) milk chocolate chips
¾ cup coarsely chopped cashews
½ cup butter, softened
½ cup sugar
2 tablespoons light corn syrup

Line 9x9-inch pan with foil. Butter foil. Spread chocolate chips evenly over bottom of pan. In saucepan, combine cashews, butter, sugar, and corn syrup. Cook over low heat, stirring constantly until butter is melted and sugar is dissolved. Continue to cook over medium heat until mixture begins to cling together and turns golden brown. Pour mixture over chocolate chips in pan, spreading evenly. Cool. Refrigerate until firm. Remove from pan. Break into pieces. Store tightly covered in cool, dry place.

Love came down at Christmas,
Love all lovely, love divine;
Love was born at Christmas,
Star and angels gave the sign.

CHRISTINA ROSSETTI

On the sixth day of Christmas
my true love sent to me:

Six Cookies a-Cooling

So Many Cookies; So Little Time!

If you've not yet gotten into the swing of a cookie exchange, now is a good time to start one. A successful gathering of this sort requires that the cookies will be of such high quality that your guests will want to come back again every year, so a few ground rules are in order. Cookies must be home-baked and fresh, and accompanied by a colorful recipe card to display with the cookies. Include in your invitation that there will be a competition for best cookie, voted on by your guests. Have attendees RSVP by phone with the cookie they plan to bring so you can avoid duplicates; ask each guest to bring two dozen cookies for display and eating, and four dozen for exchanging. They will love taking home a nice variety and supply of cookies!

Hold your exchange on a Saturday afternoon or any evening after dinner. This will allow your friends to bake cookies fresh on Saturday morning or just after work. Encourage everyone to bring their exchange cookies in a Tupperware container or cookie tin for easy transport of exchange cookies back home. Have some small zippered bags available to separate cookies with strong flavors. You'll need to bring out your largest party platters for cookie display, or invite guests to provide their own displays if they choose.

Make hot and cold drinks available: coffee, tea, punch, eggnog, cold milk, and ice water are only a few suggestions. Wassail or hot cider may be kept simmering in a slow cooker and is a festive addition to any Christmas gathering. This is a perfect opportunity to use glass plate/cup combo party dishes if you own or can borrow them, and a punch bowl set out among the cookies makes a lovely presentation.

Serve right off your dining table. Use a colorful and festive tablecloth, and put some thought and creativity into your centerpiece: a nativity scene is always a good choice or shop your local craft and hobby store for miniature buildings to create a Christmas village, or a Santa's sleigh filled with tiny wrapped gifts nestled among evergreens. Even a poinsettia or two with a pretty bow attached will add flair if you're short on time.

If your table is large enough, reserve one end for drink service. Keep an eye on this, as drinks often need replenishing. Serve coffee or tea from insulated carafes, and use pitchers (if you are not using a punch bowl) for cold drinks. Paper napkins are fine for this kind of event, but make sure they're cocktail size and holiday themed.

Encourage your guests to sit anywhere they're comfortable or want to form small chat groups. It's just fine if they fan out to different areas: hearth room, kitchen table or island, living room or the stairs.

To add some fun, have a competition for the most interesting or outlandish Christmas earrings. Place strips of colorful Christmas stationery and a few pens in a decorated Christmas basket and place it in an obvious location. Remind guests to vote sometime during the party for best earrings and favorite cookie recipe. Present prizes for each winner: a baker's apron, a new cookie sheet, or Christmas cookie cookbook for the recipe winner; a pretty necklace, bracelet, or scarf for the earring winner.

Effortless Entertaining Tips:

*Always offer a pitcher of ice water at any event. It is a beverage many people prefer, and will nicely supplement any other drinks you offer.

*Remind those bringing frosted cookies to allow drying time so they don't get smudged in packing and transport.

*Clear the coat rack or entry closet of your family's outerwear and make room for guests' coats, scarves, and purses.

> Joy to the world, the Lord is come!
> Let earth receive her King;
> Let every heart prepare Him room,
> And heaven and nature sing. . .
>
> ISAAC WATTS

Pecan Tassies

½ cup butter
1 (3 ounce) package cream
  cheese
1 cup flour

Filling:
¾ cup brown sugar
1 egg, well beaten
1 tablespoon butter, melted
1 teaspoon vanilla extract
Pinch salt
¾ to 1 cup pecans, chopped

In bowl, cream together butter and cream cheese. Add flour, and refrigerate dough 1 hour. Form into 24 small balls and press into small muffin tins; set aside. In bowl, combine all filling ingredients and pour filling into cookie shells. Bake at 350 degrees for 25 minutes.

Chocolate Snowballs

1¼ cups butter
⅔ cup granulated sugar
1 teaspoon vanilla extract
2 cups flour
⅛ teaspoon salt
½ cup cocoa powder, unsweetened
2 cups pecans, chopped
½ cup powdered sugar

In medium bowl, cream butter and granulated sugar until light and fluffy. Stir in vanilla. Sift into bowl, flour, salt, and cocoa; stir into creamed mixture. Mix in pecans until well blended. Cover dough, and chill for at least 2 hours. Preheat oven to 350 degrees. Roll chilled dough into 1-inch balls. Place balls on ungreased cookie sheet about 2 inches apart. Bake for 20 minutes in preheated oven. Roll cookies in powdered sugar when cooled.

Plum Jam Cookies

8 ounces butter
1 cup brown sugar, packed
1 egg
¼ cup water
3 cups flour
1 pinch salt
1 teaspoon baking powder
1 cup plum (or any other flavor) jam

In large bowl, cream together butter and brown sugar. Beat in egg and water. Sift together flour, salt, and baking powder; stir into butter mixture until well blended. On lightly floured surface, roll out dough to ¼-inch thickness. Cut with 2-inch round cookie cutter. Place half the cookies on baking sheet and spread ½ teaspoon plum jam in center of each one. With thimble, or small cookie cutter, cut center out of remaining cookies. Place these rounds on top of jam-topped cookies to make sandwiches. Press together. Bake cookies at 375 degrees for 10 minutes; remove to rack to cool.

Brown Sugar Cookies

    2 cups light brown sugar
    1 cup butter, melted
    3 eggs
    ¼ cup milk
    1 tablespoon vanilla extract
    1 teaspoon baking soda
    5 to 5½ cups flour

In large bowl, mix all ingredients in order given, adding just enough of the flour to make dough firm enough to roll. On lightly floured surface, roll dough out to ⅛-inch thickness. Cut into shapes as desired. Decorate with colored sugars or sprinkle lightly with brown sugar. Bake at 350 degrees for 8 to 10 minutes or until edges are lightly browned.

French Christmas Cookies

    ½ cup butter or shortening, softened
    ¾ cup sugar
    ½ cup honey
    2 egg yolks
    ¼ cup milk
    1 teaspoon vanilla extract
    3 cups flour, sifted

In bowl, cream together butter or shortening and sugar until light and fluffy. Add honey and egg yolks, beating well after each addition. Add milk and vanilla, blending well. Add flour in small amounts, stirring well after each addition. Chill dough for 2 hours. Roll out to ⅛-inch thickness on lightly floured board. Cut into desired shapes and bake on ungreased cookie sheet at 375 degrees for 10 minutes. Cool; frost if desired. Yield: 3 dozen.

Chocolate Holiday Cookies

⅔ cup powdered sugar
½ cup butter or margarine, softened
½ teaspoon vanilla extract
1 cup flour
2 tablespoons cocoa
⅛ teaspoon salt

In bowl, beat together powdered sugar, butter or margarine, and vanilla at medium speed. Reduce speed and add flour, cocoa, and salt. Divide dough in half, refrigerating second half until ready to use. Using one half at a time, place dough between sheets of lightly floured waxed paper and roll out to ⅛-inch thickness. Remove top piece of waxed paper and cut dough with 2- to 2½-inch cookie cutters. Place on ungreased cookie sheet. Bake at 325 degrees for 14 to 18 minutes. Repeat process with second half of dough. Cool cookies completely before decorating with icing (recipe follows) as desired. Yield: about 2 dozen.

Icing:
1¼ cups powdered sugar
1 tablespoon meringue powder
2 tablespoons warm water
¼ teaspoon cream of tartar

In bowl, combine all icing ingredients and beat at low speed just until moistened. Increase speed and beat until mixture is stiff and glossy. Add more warm water if icing becomes too stiff. Cover with damp paper towel until ready to use.

Butterfinger Cookies

¾ cup sugar
½ cup butter, softened
1 large egg
1 ¾ cups flour
¾ teaspoon baking soda
¼ teaspoon salt
1 cup (about three 2.1-ounce bars) Butterfinger candy bars,
   coarsely chopped

Beat sugar and butter in large mixing bowl until creamy. Beat in egg. In separate bowl, combine flour, baking soda, and salt; gradually beat into egg mixture. Stir in Butterfinger pieces. Drop dough by slightly rounded tablespoons onto ungreased baking sheet. Bake at 375 degrees for 10 to 12 minutes or until lightly browned. Cool cookies on baking sheet for 2 minutes before removing.

Cookies in a Jiffy

1 (9 ounce) box yellow cake mix
⅔ cup quick-cooking oats
½ cup butter or margarine, melted
1 egg
½ cup M&Ms or butterscotch chips

In mixing bowl, combine first four ingredients and beat well. Stir in M&Ms or butterscotch chips. Drop by tablespoonfuls 2 inches apart onto ungreased baking sheet. Bake at 350 degrees for 10 to 12 minutes or until lightly browned. Immediately remove cookies to wire racks to cool. Yield: 2 dozen.

Pumpkin Drops

2 cups butter, softened
2 cups sugar
1 (16 ounce) can pumpkin puree
2 eggs
4 cups flour
2 teaspoons pumpkin pie spice
1 teaspoon baking powder
½ teaspoon baking soda
1 (12 ounce) package white chocolate chips
1 (16 ounce) tub cream cheese frosting
¼ cup packed brown sugar

Preheat oven to 375 degrees. Grease cookie sheet. In large bowl with electric mixer at medium speed, beat butter and sugar until light and fluffy. Add pumpkin and eggs; beat until well blended. Add flour, pumpkin pie spice, baking powder, and baking soda; beat just until blended. Stir in white chocolate chips. Drop dough by teaspoonfuls about 2 inches apart onto prepared cookie sheet. Bake for 16 minutes or until cookies are set and bottoms are browned. Cool for 1 minute before removing cookies to wire racks to cool completely. While cookies are still warm, combine frosting and brown sugar in small bowl. Spread on warm cookies.

Buttermilk Cookies

3½ cups flour
1 teaspoon salt
1 teaspoon baking soda
1 teaspoon baking powder
1 cup butter or margarine, softened
2 cups sugar
2 eggs
1 cup buttermilk
Milk
Colored sugar

In small bowl, blend flour, salt, baking soda, and baking powder; set aside. In large mixing bowl, cream together butter or margarine and sugar. Add eggs and beat well. In small amounts, mix in dry ingredients, alternating with buttermilk. Cover and chill dough for at least 2 hours. Drop by teaspoonfuls onto greased cookie sheet. Dip bottom of drinking glass into milk and slightly flatten each cookie. Sprinkle with colored sugar. Bake at 350 degrees for 8 to 10 minutes.

Instant Pudding Cookies

½ cup margarine, softened
½ cup sugar
1 (3.4 ounce) package instant pudding
2 eggs, slightly beaten
1½ cups flour
½ teaspoon baking soda
¼ teaspoon salt
Nuts (optional)

Cream together margarine and sugar. Add pudding mix, eggs, flour, baking soda, and salt. Mix together well. Add nuts, if desired. Drop by teaspoonfuls onto ungreased baking sheet. Bake at 350 degrees for 12 minutes or until lightly browned. If desired, cookies may be frosted once cooled. Yield: 3 dozen.

Hazelnut Meringue Cookies

2 egg whites
½ cup sugar
⅛ teaspoon salt
½ teaspoon vanilla
½ teaspoon vinegar
1 cup hazelnuts

Line cookie sheets with either brown paper or parchment paper. Beat egg whites until soft peaks form. Gradually add sugar and salt; continue beating for 3 to 4 minutes until meringue is very stiff and sugar has dissolved. Beat in vanilla and vinegar. Fold in hazelnuts. Drop by spoonfuls in small mounds (about 1½ inches) on prepared cookie sheets. Bake at 300 sdegrees for 30 minutes or until light brown. Turn off heat. Leave in oven until oven is cool or overnight to thoroughly

Oatmeal Drop Cookies

2 cups flour
1½ cups sugar
1 teaspoon baking powder
½ teaspoon baking soda
½ teaspoon salt
1 teaspoon cinnamon
3 cups rolled oats
1 cup raisins
¾ to 1 cup semisweet chocolate chips (optional)
1 cup oil
2 eggs
½ cup milk

In large bowl, sift together flour, sugar, baking powder, baking soda, salt, and cinnamon. Mix in oats, raisins, and, if desired, chocolate chips. Add oil, eggs, and milk. Mix until thoroughly blended. Drop by teaspoonfuls onto ungreased cookie sheet. Bake at 375 degrees for 10 minutes. Yield: 6 dozen.

Chocolate Drop Cookies

½ cup shortening
2 squares unsweetened baking chocolate
2 eggs
1 cup sugar
½ teaspoon vanilla extract
1⅓ cups flour

Preheat oven to 400 degrees. Melt shortening and chocolate together in medium saucepan. Remove from heat. In bowl, beat eggs; add sugar and whisk together well. Add melted chocolate mixture, vanilla, and flour to egg mixture. Mix well. Drop by heaping tablespoons onto ungreased cookie sheet. Bake for 6 minutes.

Old-Fashioned Snickerdoodles

½ cup butter or margarine
¾ cup sugar
1 medium egg
1 teaspoon baking powder
¼ teaspoon salt
1⅔ cups flour
2½ tablespoons sugar mixed with 1½ teaspoons cinnamon

Preheat oven to 400 degrees. Combine butter or margarine with sugar in large bowl. Add egg and beat until creamy. Add baking powder, salt, and flour. Stir until mixture forms thick dough. Put cinnamon-sugar mixture in small bowl. Shape dough into 1-inch balls. Roll balls in cinnamon-sugar mixture. Place on greased cookie sheet. Using bottom of cup, press balls to flatten slightly. Bake for 10 minutes.

Perfect Pumpkin Cookies

2½ cups flour
1 teaspoon baking powder
1 teaspoon baking soda
½ teaspoon salt
2 teaspoons cinnamon
½ teaspoon nutmeg
¼ teaspoon cloves
½ cup butter, softened
1 cup brown sugar
1 (16 ounce) can pumpkin
  puree
1 egg
1 teaspoon vanilla extract

Icing:
2 cups powdered sugar
3 tablespoons milk
1 tablespoon butter
1 teaspoon vanilla extract

Preheat oven to 350 degrees. In large bowl, combine flour, baking powder, baking soda, salt, and spices. Mix well with whisk; set aside. In separate bowl, cream butter and sugar; add pumpkin, egg, and vanilla, and beat until creamy. Mix in dry ingredients. Drop on cookie sheet by spoonfuls and flatten slightly with palm of hand. Bake for 15 to 20 minutes. Icing: In bowl, combine powdered sugar, milk, butter, and vanilla. Add more milk as needed for consistency. Allow cookies to cool, then drizzle icing with fork over top of cookies.

Angel Cookies

1 angel food cake mix
½ cup water
1 (8 to 12 ounce) bag dried mixed fruit, finely chopped

In bowl, combine cake mix and water. Stir in fruit. Line cookie sheet with foil. Drop dough by teaspoonfuls on foil. Bake at 400 degrees for 8 to 10 minutes until puffy and golden in color. Cool cookies well before trying to remove from foil.

Old-Fashioned Preserve Thumbprints

1 (8 ounce) package cream cheese, softened
¾ cup butter, softened
1 cup powdered sugar
2¼ cups flour
½ teaspoon baking soda
½ cup chopped pecans
½ teaspoon vanilla extract
Strawberry and peach preserves

In bowl, beat cream cheese, butter, and powdered sugar until smooth. Add flour and baking soda, stirring to blend well. Add pecans and vanilla; mix well. Cover and chill dough for at least 30 minutes. Preheat oven to 350 degrees. Shape dough into 1-inch balls. Place on ungreased cookie sheet. Press thumb in middle of each cookie; fill imprint with about 1 teaspoon preserves. Bake for 14 to 16 minutes or until light golden brown. Cool on wire rack. Yield: 3 dozen.

Chocolate Caramel Cookies

3 cups flour
½ cup cocoa
3 sticks salted butter, softened
1 cup sugar
1 egg
1 teaspoon vanilla extract
1 (12 ounce) package semisweet chocolate chips
1 cup finely chopped pecans, toasted
1 bottle caramel ice-cream topping

Chocolate drizzle:
½ cup semisweet chocolate chips, melted
2 teaspoons shortening

Preheat oven to 350 degrees. In bowl, whisk together flour and cocoa; set aside.
In separate bowl, cream together butter and sugar. Beat in egg and vanilla.
Gradually add flour mixture. Stir in chocolate chips and pecans. Roll dough
into 1-inch balls and place on ungreased cookie sheet. Press thumb in center
of each ball. Fill each indentation half full with caramel topping. Bake for 15 to
18 minutes. Let cookies set for 5 minutes before removing from cookie sheet.
Chocolate drizzle: In microwave-safe bowl, melt chocolate chips and shortening
on medium-high for 1 to 2 minutes. Stir until smooth. With fork, drizzle
chocolate over cookies. Yield: 5 dozen.

Oatmeal Scotchies

¾ cup butter, softened
¾ cup granulated sugar
¾ cup brown sugar
2 eggs
1 teaspoon vanilla extract
1½ cups flour
1 teaspoon baking soda
1 teaspoon cinnamon
½ teaspoon salt
3 cups rolled oats
2 cups butterscotch chips

Preheat oven to 375 degrees. In mixing bowl, beat butter and sugars together. Add eggs and vanilla, beating well. In separate bowl, combine dry ingredients with whisk until well blended. Gradually add to creamy mixture and stir until blended. Stir in oats and butterscotch chips. Drop spoonfuls of dough onto ungreased cookie sheet. Bake for 7 to 9 minutes or until edges begin to brown. Store cookies in sealed container. Yield: 4 dozen.

Blessed is the season which engages the whole world in a conspiracy of love.

HAMILTON WRIGHT MABIE

On the seventh day of Christmas
my true love sent to me:

Seven Desserts a-Delighting

Happy Birthday, Jesus!

This one is for the kids. Invite as many as you can handle, and encourage parents to deliver and pick up their children promptly, but ask one or two dads or moms ahead of time to stay and help out if you need them.

Ask each child to bring along a baked Christmas dessert in a disposable container. Stress that these are for a local retirement center. You need only turn them over to the staff at the home and ask them to put them out as a buffet or in any other manner they choose. Make or buy a large Christmas greeting card on which each child can sign, draw a picture, or write a message. Elderly people will be blessed by looking at it throughout the holidays, and they'll love the dessert buffet!

Decorate your table just as you would for any very special birthday party. Go all out with balloons, streamers, party hats, noisemakers, party plates and napkins, and, of course, ice cream. Bake a cake (try the Red Velvet recipe in this section). Use as many candles as there are attendees, and remind the children that Jesus' birth made it possible for us to be reborn! Then gather the kids around to sing "Happy Birthday" to Jesus and blow out the candles together.

A nativity is an excellent choice for a centerpiece. Place it right in the center of the festivities. If you have one small enough for your table, use it as a reminder of the setting of Christ's birth. Another idea that might get even more attention is to build a wooden crèche and place a swaddled baby doll in it with hay or straw for bedding. Read a short, modern version of the Christmas story while the kids are seated. You may want to have a book with vivid pictures to show as you read.

The kids will enjoy playing "Musical Chairs" to Christmas music or "Fill the Stocking," which has the guests form two teams lined up across the room from two hung Christmas stockings. A bowl of wrapped candy and a spoon are placed at the head of each line. In relay fashion, the children take turns carrying a candy on the spoon, depositing it in the stocking and running back to hand the spoon off to the next person in line. "Christmas Twenty Questions" is played by everyone sitting in a circle around a bowl of candy. (One of those you used in the relay game.) Going around the circle, kids take turns asking the hostess 2 or 3 questions and then taking a guess about a list of simple things or people pertaining to the Christmas season. When anyone guesses correctly, he gets to choose a candy from the bowl. Let every child choose a candy when the game is over.

As the party comes to a close, join hands in a circle and sing a Christmas carol or other seasonal song together. Children love to sing!

Favor: Send each child home with a brightly wrapped popcorn ball or bundle fruit roll-ups and tie with a Christmas ribbon.

Effortless Entertaining Tips:

*Serve a light, kid-friendly, protein-rich snack ahead of cake and ice cream
   (chicken nuggets or drumsticks, hot dogs or grilled cheese sandwiches).
*Avoid sugary drinks. Offer water or milk instead.
*Keep the party to about two hours.

> *Unto us a Son is given!*
> *He has come from God's own heaven,*
> *Bringing with Him, from above,*
> *Holy peace and holy love.*
>
> HORATIUS BONAR

Chocolate Truffle Cake

1 (12 ounce) package semisweet chocolate chips, divided
½ cup heavy whipping cream
4 eggs
½ cup sugar
¼ cup flour
1 cup frozen whipped topping, thawed

Preheat oven to 325 degrees. Reserving ⅛ cup chocolate chips, place remaining chips in large microwavable bowl. Add cream. Microwave on high for 2 minutes or until chocolate is almost melted. Stir until chocolate is completely melted; cool slightly. Add eggs, sugar, and flour; beat with whisk until well blended. Pour into lightly greased 9-inch pie pan. Bake for 35 minutes or until outer sides of pie are puffed and center is slightly soft; cool. Top with whipped topping just before serving.

Cheese Danish

2 (8 ounce) cans refrigerated crescent roll dough
2 (8 ounce) packages cream cheese, softened
½ cup granulated sugar
1 teaspoon vanilla extract
1 stick butter or margarine
1 teaspoon cinnamon
½ cup brown sugar

Unroll 1 package of rolls onto bottom of ungreased 9x13-inch pan. Pat seams closed. In bowl, beat cream cheese, granulated sugar, and vanilla until smooth. Spread over dough. Unroll second package of crescent rolls over top of cheese mixture, patting seams closed. Melt butter or margarine with cinnamon and pour over top. Sprinkle with brown sugar and bake at 350 degrees for 30 to 35 minutes.

Chocolate Pecan Pie

1 ½ cups coarsely chopped pecans
1 cup semisweet chocolate chips
1 (8 inch) pie shell, partially baked
½ cup light corn syrup
½ cup sugar
2 eggs, lightly beaten
¼ cup butter, melted

Preheat oven to 325 degrees. Sprinkle pecans and chocolate chips into pie shell. In a mixing bowl, combine corn syrup, sugar, eggs, and butter. Mix well. Slowly pour mixture over pecans and chocolate. Bake for 1 hour.

Red Velvet Cake

3 teaspoons unsweetend cocoa powder
½ ounce red food coloring
½ cup shortening
1½ cups sugar
2 eggs
1 teaspoon vanilla extract
2 cups flour
½ teaspoon salt
1 cup buttermilk
1 teaspoon baking soda
1 teaspoon vinegar

Preheat oven to 350 degrees. In large bowl, make paste with cocoa and food coloring. Cream in shortening and sugar. Add eggs one at a time, mixing well after each. Stir in vanilla. In separate bowl, sift together flour and salt. Add flour to cocoa mixture in small amounts, alternating with buttermilk. In small bowl, dissolve baking soda in vinegar then add to batter, blending well. Bake in cake pan(s) of choice for 25 to 35 minutes or until toothpick inserted in center comes out clean.

White Chocolate Cheesecake

3 (8 ounce) packages cream cheese, softened
¾ cup sugar
¼ cup flour
3 eggs
4 ounces white chocolate
½ teaspoon vanilla extract
1½ cups heavy whipping cream

Preheat oven to 300 degrees. Wrap outside of 10-inch springform pan with foil. Grease inside of pan. In mixing bowl, beat cream cheese, sugar, and flour until light and fluffy. Beat in eggs one at a time, mixing well after each addition. Scrape bowl. Melt white chocolate. With electric mixer on low speed, mix melted white chocolate into cream cheese mixture. Slowly beat in vanilla and cream. Blend well. Pour mixture into prepared springform pan. Place pan in larger baking dish filled with warm water, being careful water does not overflow into pan. Bake for 50 to 60 minutes or until center of cheesecake is just firm. Cool at room temperature for 1 hour. Refrigerate until set before removing from pan.

Chocolate Pound Cake

1 box chocolate cake mix
1 small box instant chocolate pudding
1¾ cups milk
2 eggs
1 bag mini chocolate chips
Powdered sugar

Preheat oven to 350 degrees. In large bowl, combine all ingredients except powdered sugar and beat by hand. Bake for 1 hour. Before serving, dust with powdered sugar.

Marble Bars

½ cup peanut butter
⅓ cup butter
¾ cup granulated sugar
¾ cup brown sugar
2 eggs
1 cup flour
1 teaspoon baking powder
¼ teaspoon salt
2 teaspoons vanilla extract
2 cups semisweet chocolate chips

Preheat oven to 350 degrees. In large bowl, cream together peanut butter, butter, and sugars; beat in eggs. Add flour, baking powder, salt, and vanilla, mixing well. Spread in greased 9x13-inch pan. Sprinkle chips over top. Bake for 5 minutes. With blade of butter knife, swirl melted chips down through batter to create marble effect. Return to oven and bake for 25 minutes or until lightly browned.

Dipped Rice Treats

¼ cup butter
4 cups mini marshmallows
6 cups crisp rice cereal
1 (12 ounce) package semisweet chocolate chips

Grease 9x13-inch dish. In large saucepan, melt butter over low heat. Add marshmallows, stirring constantly until melted and smooth. Remove from heat. Stir in cereal. With buttered fingers, press mixture into pan. Cool. Cut into squares. Melt chocolate chips in small saucepan over low heat. Dip squares halfway into chocolate. Place on waxed paper to cool.

Lemon Tarts

½ cup butter
2 cups sugar
2 lemons, zest and juice
4 eggs
24 mini tart shells, baked

Melt butter and sugar in double boiler. Add zest, then beat in eggs and lemon juice. Boil to thicken. Spoon into baked tart shells. Cool.

Caramel Cashew Bars

Rhodes Texas rolls, thawed and raised
1½ cups chocolate chips
14 ounces caramels, unwrapped
⅓ cup evaporated milk
⅓ cup butter
1⅔ cups powdered sugar
2 cups cashew halves
½ cup semisweet chocolate chips

Press risen dough of 4 rolls together and roll into 9x13-inch rectangle. Place in 9x13-inch pan sprayed with nonstick cooking spray. Sprinkle with 1½ cups chocolate chips. Repeat roll layer with remaining 4 rolls and place over top of chocolate chips. Bake at 350 degrees for 15 minutes. Let cool. Place caramels, milk, and butter in medium saucepan. Melt on low heat, stirring occasionally until smooth. Remove from heat. Add powdered sugar and stir until smooth. Fold in cashews. Pour mixture over baked crust. Melt ½ cup chocolate chips in microwave, and drizzle over caramel layer. Refrigerate until firm, and cut into squares.

Double-Chocolate Mud Bars

½ cup butter, softened
1 cup granulated sugar
2 large eggs, separated
1½ cups flour
1 teaspoon baking powder
½ teaspoon salt
1 cup walnuts, chopped
½ cup semisweet chocolate chips
1 cup mini marshmallows
1 cup M&Ms (optional)
1 cup brown sugar, firmly packed

In large bowl, cream together butter and sugar. Add egg yolks one at a time, stirring well after each. In separate bowl, mix together flour, baking powder, and salt. Fold flour mixture into sugar mixture. Press mixture into greased 9x13-inch baking pan. Pack down firmly. Sprinkle walnuts, chocolate chips, marshmallows, and M&Ms, if desired, over top of mixture in pan. In mixing bowl, beat egg whites at high speed until stiff peaks form. Fold in brown sugar. Spread over mixture in pan. Bake 35 minutes at 350 degrees. Cool completely; cut into squares.

Peanut Butter Pie

1 (8 ounce) package cream cheese, softened
1 cup powdered sugar
1 cup peanut butter
1 (12 ounce) container whipped topping
1 graham cracker piecrust

In large bowl, mix all ingredients except piecrust, reserving small amount of whipped topping to top pie, if desired. Pour mixture into graham cracker crust. Refrigerate until ready to serve.

Angel Cake Surprise

1 (10 inch tube pan) angel food cake or pound cake
1 (3 ounce) box strawberry-flavored gelatin
1 (15 ounce) can sliced peaches
3 bananas
1 (20 ounce) can crushed pineapple, drained (optional)
1 (5 ounce) package instant vanilla pudding mix
1 (8 ounce) container frozen whipped topping, thawed

Break angel food or pound cake into bite-size pieces. Put into 9x13-inch pan (preferably glass). In bowl, dissolve gelatin in 1 cup hot water and pour over cake pieces, spreading to edges of pan. Reserving juice, drain peaches into separate bowl; pour juice over gelatin in pan. Slice bananas on top of gelatin. Arrange peach slices over banana slices. If desired, add crushed pineapple over top of peaches. Prepare instant pudding according to instructions on box and pour evenly over fruit. Spread whipped topping on top of pudding. Try to keep layers separate. Refrigerate at least 2 hours before serving.

Kentucky Derby Pie

4 eggs, beaten
½ cup butter, melted
¾ cup brown sugar
1 cup light corn syrup
1 cup chocolate chips
1 cup pecans, chopped
1 teaspoon vanilla extract
1 teaspoon flour
1 unbaked pie shell

In large bowl, mix all ingredients and pour into pie shell. Bake at 350 degrees for 40 to 45 minutes.

Christmas Cake in a Snap

1 box white cake mix
Red and green food coloring
Icing
Cake decorations (candy pieces, sprinkles, etc.)

Prepare cake as directed on box. Divide batter into two bowls. Add red food coloring to one bowl and green food coloring to the other. Bake in two layer pans. When cakes are cool, slice each cake in half lengthwise so you have 4 thin cakes. Whip up your favorite white icing. Alternate colored layers with icing. Decorate cake with candy and sprinkles.

Candy Bar Squares

¾ cup butter or margarine, softened
¼ cup peanut butter
1 cup brown sugar, packed
1 teaspoon baking soda
2 cups quick-cooking oats
1½ cups flour
1 egg
1 (14 ounce) can sweetened condensed milk (not evaporated)
4 cups candy bars, chopped (for example, Snickers or Milky Way)

Preheat oven to 350 degrees. In large bowl, combine butter or margarine and peanut butter. Add brown sugar and baking soda; mix well. Stir in oats and flour. In separate bowl, reserve 1¾ cups crumb mixture; set aside. Stir egg into remaining crumb mixture; press firmly on bottom of ungreased 15x10x1-inch baking pan. Bake 15 minutes. Spread sweetened condensed milk over baked crust. Stir together reserved crumb mixture and candy bar pieces; sprinkle evenly over top. Bake 25 minutes or until golden. Cool. Cut into bars. Store covered at room temperature.

Pull-Apart Bread

4 (8 ounce) cans refrigerated biscuits
1½ cups granulated sugar, divided
2 teaspoons cinnamon
⅓ cup brown sugar
1 cup butter
¼ cup semisweet chocolate chips

Preheat oven to 350 degrees. Cut biscuits into quarters. In bowl, combine ¾ cup sugar with cinnamon. Roll each piece of biscuit in cinnamon-sugar mixture. Place on bottom of greased Bundt pan. In saucepan, slowly bring remaining ¾ cup sugar, brown sugar, butter, and chocolate chips to boil. Remove from heat. Pour over biscuits in pan. Bake for 30 to 45 minutes. Invert pan onto serving dish and serve immediately.

Miniature Cheesecakes

2 eggs
2 (8 ounce) packages cream cheese, softened
½ cup sugar
1 teaspoon vanilla extract
3 cups graham cracker crumbs
1 can cherry pie filling

In mixing bowl, beat first four ingredients until smooth. Line miniature muffin pans with paper liners. Spoon 1 tablespoon graham cracker crumbs into each muffin cup. Top each cup ¾ full with mixture. Bake at 350 degrees for 15 minutes. When cool, top each with one cherry from can of cherry pie filling. Yield: 48 cheesecakes.

The joy of brightening other lives, bearing each others' burdens, easing others' loads and supplanting empty hearts and lives with generous gifts becomes for us the magic of Christmas.

W. C. Jones

On the eighth day of Christmas
my true love sent to me:

Eight Kids a-Cooking

Kids' Luncheon

Invite your friends to bring their kids to a Saturday afternoon charity luncheon. Each guest should bring a Christmas-wrapped shoebox packed with items a homeless person would value. Suggest that they choose items that they would find useful were they to find themselves in a homeless situation, including hygiene articles, small items of clothing, nonperishable food, gift certificates, or even small amounts of cash. Also ask each family to bring an unopened plastic gallon jug of vitamin-rich fruit juice.

This luncheon with a heart is a great idea for kids and their parents. Shopping for the gifts and packing the shoeboxes provide many teachable moments. The hostess's job will be, within a day or two, to deliver the boxes and juice to a local homeless shelter.

For luncheon table décor, create a centerpiece that will remind guests of the simple outdoor life. Arrange supermarket daisies in a campfire coffeepot. Keep lunch fare uncomplicated by choosing from any of the kid-friendly recipes in this section. Children usually enjoy helping in the kitchen, so let the kids have some fun making one of the recipes together with their parents for lunch. Provide the makings of s'mores for dessert, allowing each guest to toast marshmallows over a stove-top burner. (This is usually forbidden at home, so the kids will love it. However, you must insist that parents hover over this process !) Provide long-handled utensils, like fondue forks or disposable wooden shish kebab holders, for this task.

Steer lunch conversation toward a discussion of the things we think we could not live without and ways we can all help meet the basic needs of those less fortunate. Focus, in particular, on the hardship of being without a roof, transportation, or loved ones during such a family-oriented time of year as Christmas. Provide brochures from local shelters or food kitchens with occasions listed where an individual or entire family can volunteer to serve. Keep the mood from becoming too somber by giving thanks, perhaps during the meal prayer, for the abundance we enjoy and for the opportunity and blessing it is to be able to share what we have with others.

Send each guest home with a small, sprouting bulb that has been potted in a soup can (make sure there are no sharp edges). Suggest these are reminders that beautiful and precious things often have very small beginnings and that a humble shoebox of help can bring immense relief and joy to those without the most basic needs. This will also serve to inspire them to let their service to the needy increase.

Effortless Entertaining Tips:

*Don't forget the graham crackers and Hershey bars for the s'mores!
*Serving lunch on paper plates is another reminder of the only "china" homeless people own.

*Once in royal David's city
Stood a lowly cattle shed,
Where a mother laid her baby
In a manger for His bed:
Mary was that mother mild,
Jesus Christ, her little child.*

CECIL FRANCES ALEXANDER

Fruit Pizza

1 (8 ounce) package refrigerated sugar cookie dough
1 (8 ounce) package cream cheese
1 (12 ounce) container whipped topping
½ cup sugar
½ teaspoon vanilla extract
Mandarin oranges
Fresh fruit of choice

Preheat oven according to directions on cookie dough package. Cut cookies in ½-inch slices and arrange on pizza pan, pressing together to make crust. Bake for 15 to 20 minutes or until done. Combine cream cheese, whipped topping, sugar, and vanilla in bowl. Stir until smooth and spread over cooled cookie crust. Arrange fruit in layers on cookie crust. Cut into pizzalike slices.

Cinnamon Biscuits

4 (8 ounce) cans refrigerator biscuits
1½ cups sugar, divided
2½ teaspoons cinnamon, divided
¾ cup butter

Preheat oven to 350 degrees. Cut each biscuit into quarters. Combine ½ cup sugar and 1 teaspoon cinnamon in bowl. Roll biscuits in cinnamon-sugar mixture, making sure they are evenly coated. Grease Bundt cake pan and place biscuit pieces in bottom of pan, keeping them evenly distributed. Combine remaining 1 cup sugar, butter, and remaining 1½ teaspoons cinnamon in small saucepan. Bring to boil. Pour over biscuits and bake for 45 minutes or until done. Let cool and flip over on plate. Pull apart to eat.

Muffins

3 eggs
1 cup milk
1 cup flour
½ teaspoon salt

Mix all ingredients in bowl. In greased muffin pan, fill each cup ½ full. Place muffins in cold oven. Heat to 450 degrees and bake for 30 minutes. Serve with jelly, jam, or preserves. Yield: 12 muffins.

Sweet Toast

12 large eggs
½ teaspoon cinnamon
2 tablespoons milk
1 loaf sliced white bread
Vegetable oil
Butter (optional)
Maple syrup (optional)
Peanut butter (optional)
Powdered sugar (optional)

In bowl, beat eggs lightly. Add cinnamon and milk. Whisk with fork. Dip bread slices in egg mixture, evenly coating both sides. Place on heated skillet coated with vegetable oil and fry until both sides of bread have browned. Serve warm, topped with butter, maple syrup, peanut butter, or powdered sugar.

Applesauce

4 apples
1 cup water
3 tablespoons honey
Ground cinnamon

Wash, core, and roughly chop apples. Cook apples and water in medium sauce-pan over medium heat until apples are tender. Add honey and stir. Pour into serving dish and sprinkle with cinnamon.

Baked Corn

¼ cup butter, melted
1 box cornbread mix
1 (15 ounce) can creamed corn
1 (15 ounce) can whole-kernel corn, drained
2 eggs, beaten
3 tablespoons milk

Preheat oven to 400 degrees. In mixing bowl, blend butter with cornbread mix.
Add both cans of corn, eggs, and milk; stir until well blended. Pour into greased
2-quart baking dish and bake for 30 minutes.

Bacon Sausage Bites

1 (16 ounce) package ready-to-serve bacon
1 package mini sausages

Preheat oven to 400 degrees. Cut bacon in half; wrap bacon around each sausage, securing bacon with wooden pick. Place on greased baking sheet and bake for 15 minutes.

Chicken Casserole

1½ cups chicken (or turkey), cooked and diced
1½ cups elbow macaroni, uncooked
1 cup cheddar cheese, shredded
1 (10½ ounce) can condensed cream of chicken soup
1 cup milk
½ teaspoon salt

Preheat oven to 350 degrees. Mix all ingredients together in bowl. Pour mixture into ungreased 2-quart casserole dish. Cover with foil and bake for 1 hour. Yield: 4 to 6 servings.

Deviled Eggs

12 eggs, hard boiled
½ teaspoon salt
1 teaspoon prepared mustard
1 teaspoon vinegar
¼ cup mayonnaise
Paprika

Cut eggs in half lengthwise. Carefully remove yolks and place in small mixing bowl. Mash yolks and blend in salt, mustard, vinegar, and mayonnaise. Fill hollowed egg whites with yolk mixture and sprinkle with paprika. Refrigerate until ready to serve.

Cranberry Fluff

1 cup cranberry juice
1 (3 ounce) box raspberry-flavored gelatin
1 cup frozen whipped topping, thawed

Bring cranberry juice to boil in medium saucepan. Remove from heat and add gelatin; stir until dissolved. Pour into 9x9-inch dish and chill until thickened. Fold in whipped topping and chill until firm.

Chili

1 pound ground beef
1 small onion, chopped
1 (16 ounce) can kidney beans, rinsed and drained
1 (14½ ounce) can stewed tomatoes
½ teaspoon salt
½ teaspoon black pepper
1½ tablespoons chili powder

Brown ground beef and onion in large skillet. Drain fat. Add remaining ingredients and cook on medium heat for 45 minutes, stirring often.

Fancy Hot Dogs

8 hot dogs
1 (8 ounce) jar grape jelly
1 (8 ounce) jar cranberry sauce

Slice hot dogs into ½-inch pieces. In saucepan, heat grape jelly and cranberry sauce over medium heat, stirring constantly until heated through. Add hot dog pieces and cook on low heat until hot dogs are hot. Serve with toothpicks.

Fruit Salad

1 (3 ounce) box strawberry-flavored gelatin
1 (14½ ounce) can fruit cocktail, drained

Prepare strawberry gelatin as directed on box. Add fruit cocktail to gelatin and stir. Pour into 9x9-inch baking dish and refrigerate until firm.

Fried Green Beans

3 cups fresh green beans
⅓ cup Italian dressing
2 tablespoons toasted almond slivers (optional)

In large skillet, sauté green beans in half the dressing until tender. Add remaining dressing to green beans and lightly toss. Pour in serving dish and sprinkle with almonds.

Pigs in a Blanket

1 (8 ounce) can refrigerated crescent roll dough
8 hot dogs

Preheat oven to 350 degrees. Flatten each triangle of crescent roll dough and wrap each around a hot dog, sealing seam as much as possible. Place on ungreased cookie sheet. Bake for 10 minutes or until dough is lightly brown.

Four-Layer Breakfast Dish

    1 pound ground sausage
    4 eggs
    ¼ cup milk
    1 (8 ounce) can refrigerated crescent roll dough
    2 to 3 cups mozzarella cheese, shredded

Preheat oven to 350 degrees. In frying pan, brown sausage; drain excess fat. In bowl, beat eggs and milk together; add sausage. Put rolls in bottom of 9x13-inch buttered casserole dish; then layer on sausage and egg mixture, and top with cheese. Bake for 30 to 50 minutes, until eggs are no longer runny.

Bacon Dip

    1 (16 ounce) container sour cream
    ½ teaspoon onion powder
    1 (16 ounce) package ready-to-serve bacon
    ½ cup cheddar cheese, shredded
    1 cup lettuce, shredded
    1 cup tomatoes, chopped

In bowl, mix sour cream and onion powder together and spread into 9-inch pie plate. Heat bacon as directed on package and cut into small pieces. Sprinkle over sour cream mixture. Top with cheese, lettuce, and tomatoes. Serve with crackers.

Cookie-Cutter Toast

1 slice bread
Butter
Peanut butter (optional)
Jelly

Toast piece of bread. Using Christmas cookie cutter, cut toast into desired shape.
Spread with butter or peanut butter and favorite jelly.

Biscuit Coffee Cake

2 (8 ounce) cans buttermilk refrigerated biscuits
⅓ cup brown sugar, firmly packed
¼ cup butter, melted
1 teaspoon cinnamon
⅓ cup pecans

Preheat oven to 350 degrees. In lightly greased 9x9-inch pan, arrange biscuits,
overlapping edges. In bowl, combine remaining ingredients and spread evenly
over biscuits. Bake for 15 minutes or until done.

Christmas. . .is not an eternal event at all, but a piece of one's home that one carries in one's heart.

FREYA STARK

On the ninth day of Christmas
my true love sent to me:

Nine Main Dishes a-Mixing

Simply Elegant Dinner Party

The elegant, seated dinner party has become less common in these days of more spontaneous and casual entertaining. Once in a while, however, people love to attend an event where the hostess has obviously pulled out all the stops and spent considerable time, effort, and expense to favor her guests with a beautiful, slow-cooked meal. Advance planning is the key to success!

Begin with your guest list; you'll need to keep the group to a size that will fit comfortably at your dining room table. Once you've decided on a date, send out a simple, pretty invitation by mail.

Next, plan the menu. Start with the main course (a meat dish), and build the meal from there. Choose a starch (potatoes, rice, or pasta), a fresh or cooked vegetable, bread, beverage, and dessert. If your meal is heavy, the dessert you choose should be light, and vice versa. Light appetizers are a good idea, since a heavy meal is soon to follow; a festive cup of punch or eggnog will suffice.

While putting together your menu, imagine how the food will look on the plate. Some color is needed to make it inviting. Does everything fit on the plate, or will you need overflow dishes? Are you planning a soup course? A salad? Think about the space on your table and what extra bowls, spoons, etc. you might need.

Sit down with pen, paper, and recipes. Build your shopping list one recipe at a time. Check your list twice. Nothing can throw a wrench into your evening like realizing at the last minute that you've forgotten an essential ingredient. Always plan to do your grocery shopping a day ahead. This ensures freshness and allows you to prepare your dishes throughout the day of the party with less stress.

Now plan your table setting and centerpiece. Make sure you have enough chairs, the right size tablecloth, coordinating cloth napkins and napkin rings if you plan to use them. Pretty napkin rings are easy to make with strips of cloth Christmas ribbon, strands of beads, or twine-covered wire with artificial Christmas sprays around each napkin. If you own Christmas china, this is the time to pull it all out and use every piece! If your set is basic, you can supplement with clear glass salad plates, bowls, and cups. They're inexpensive to purchase at dollar and discount stores.

A low centerpiece is crucial as your guests will be doing most of their visiting while seated at the table and should be able to see each other easily. Fresh-cut flowers, floating candles among flower petals or cranberries, or short evergreen sprays with bright Christmas bulbs attached are all good choices. Candlelight is a must, but don't go overboard, and avoid buying scented candles that can overwhelm and interfere with the taste and smell of the food. Turn overhead lights down, but don't make your guests squint to see what's being passed to them! A lamp placed in the corner of the dining room, or set atop the buffet, will provide plenty of soft light.

Don't rush things. As guests arrive, allow them to chat and warm up over appetizers. Plan to serve dinner about 30 minutes after everyone gets there. Count on it—someone will be late. Place cards are an elegant touch and help avoid seating stall and confusion. Using card stock, cut cards to about 2x3 inches. Scroll first names only with a black calligraphy pen. Tuck them into the spines of pine cones and place them at each setting. Steer dinner conversation away from politics, doctrine, or gossip; plan ahead to subtly introduce lively, pleasant topics if needed.

Provide decaf coffee and tea with dessert, but have it set up ahead and ready to hit the start button as you prepare to serve dessert. Have backup coffee filter and grounds ready to go for a second pot. Set up cream, sugar, and dessert dishes in advance, all ready to go when dinner dishes are removed.

Effortless Entertaining Tips:

*Set the table the evening before, so if you're missing something crucial you'll know it ahead of time.

*Choose relaxing Christmas music, and have it ready to turn on when guests arrive.

*Light the candles, sit down, and close your eyes for 10 minutes ahead of guests' arrival. If you're rested and relaxed, they will be, too.

Beef Burgundy

2 tablespoons olive oil
1½ to 2 pounds cubed beef stew meat
½ cup chopped onion
1 (10 ounce) can condensed cream of mushroom soup
¼ cup red wine vinegar
¼ cup reduced-salt beef broth
¼ teaspoon garlic powder
1 cup sliced fresh mushrooms
Egg noodles or rice, prepared

Heat oil in skillet. Add stew meat and brown. Remove meat from pan; set aside. Add onion to pan and sauté until tender. In ovenproof casserole dish, mix meat, onion, soup, vinegar, broth, and garlic powder. Bake, covered, at 325 degrees for 3 hours. Just before the last 20 minutes of baking time, add mushrooms and return casserole to oven. Serve over egg noodles or rice. Yield: 4 to 6 servings.

Country Holiday Ham

1 (7 pound) sugar-cured ham
Whole cloves
2 cups maple pancake syrup
½ cup cola

Preheat oven to 350 degrees. Remove skin from ham. Score fat surface of ham with knife in diamond shape or other design, and stud with cloves. Pour syrup then cola over ham. Cover with foil, and bake for 3 to 4 hours, checking after 3 hours to make sure ham isn't getting dry.

Hot Turkey Salad

3 cups diced cooked turkey
4 hard-boiled eggs, chopped
2 cups diced celery
1 cup sliced fresh mushrooms
2 tablespoons diced onion
¾ cup mayonnaise
1 tablespoon lemon juice
½ cup cornflake crumbs
2 tablespoons butter or margarine, melted

In large bowl, combine turkey, eggs, celery, mushrooms, onion, mayonnaise, and lemon juice. Transfer to 9x13-inch baking dish. Top with cornflake crumbs and drizzle with melted butter or margarine. Bake at 350 degrees for 30 minutes. Yield: 6 to 8 servings.

Porcupine Meatballs

1 (10 ounce) can condensed tomato soup
1 pound ground beef
½ cup uncooked white rice
½ cup water
1 teaspoon salt
½ teaspoon black pepper
1 small onion, minced
½ tablespoon dried parsley flakes
1 teaspoon Worcestershire sauce

In bowl, mix tomato soup with one soup can of water. Set aside. In large mixing bowl, combine remaining ingredients. Form meat mixture into 1½-inch balls. Place meatballs in greased casserole dish. Pour soup and water mixture over meatballs. Cover and bake at 350 degrees for 45 minutes. Yield: 4 servings.

Home-Style Roast Beef

1 (10 to 12 pound) bottom round beef roast
1 (14½ ounce) can chicken broth
1 (10¼ ounce) can beef gravy
1 (10¾ ounce) can condensed cream of celery soup
¼ cup water
¼ cup Worcestershire sauce
¼ cup soy sauce
3 tablespoons dried parsley flakes
3 tablespoons dried dill weed
2 tablespoons dried thyme
4½ teaspoons garlic powder
1 teaspoon celery salt
1 teaspoon black pepper
1 large onion, sliced into rings

Place roast in large roasting pan, fat side up. Prick meat with meat fork. In bowl, combine broth, gravy, soup, water, Worcestershire, and soy sauce. Pour mixture evenly over roast, then sprinkle roast with seasonings. Place onion rings over roast. Bake, uncovered, at 325 degrees for 2½ to 3½ hours or until meat reaches desired doneness. Meat thermometer should read 140 degrees for rare roast, 160 degrees for medium roast, and 170 degrees for well-done roast. Let roast stand

Oven-Fried Chicken

¼ cup butter or margarine, melted and divided
⅓ cup cornmeal
⅓ cup flour
¼ teaspoon paprika
¼ teaspoon salt
¼ teaspoon garlic powder
2 tablespoons grated Parmesan cheese
4 to 6 boneless, skinless chicken breasts

Pour half of melted butter or margarine in 9x13-inch baking dish and set aside. Combine next 6 ingredients in sealed plastic bag. Shake each piece of chicken in mixture to coat. Place chicken pieces in baking dish, and pour remaining butter over chicken. Bake at 350 degrees for 1 hour and 15 minutes. Yield: 4 to 6 servings.

Cranberry Chicken

6 boneless, skinless chicken breast halves
1 can whole-berry cranberry sauce
1 large Granny Smith apple, peeled and diced
½ cup raisins
1 teaspoon orange peel
¼ cup walnuts, chopped
1 teaspoon curry powder
1 teaspoon cinnamon

Place chicken in greased 9x13-inch baking dish. Bake at 350 degrees for 20 minutes. While chicken is cooking, combine remaining ingredients in bowl. Spoon cranberry mixture over chicken. Return to oven for 20 to 25 minutes more or until chicken juices run clear.

Sweet-and-Sour Chops

4 loin-cut pork chops, excess fat trimmed
4 medium potatoes, cut into ¾-inch slices
2 (10 ounce) cans condensed cream of mushroom soup
1 small onion, diced
1 garlic clove, minced
3 tablespoons honey
3 tablespoons prepared mustard
3 tablespoons lemon juice
½ teaspoon Worcestershire sauce
½ teaspoon dried parsley flakes
½ teaspoon ground sage
½ teaspoon ground thyme
Salt and pepper to taste

In large skillet, quickly brown pork chops on both sides. Place pork chops in large baking dish and set aside. Boil potatoes in salted water until slightly softened. Drain well, and layer over pork chops. In large bowl, combine remaining ingredients; stir until thoroughly combined. Pour mixture over potatoes and chops. Bake at 350 degrees for 25 to 30 minutes or until pork chops are done. Yield: 4 servings.

Mainstay Macaroni Casserole

4 tablespoons butter
4 tablespoons flour
¼ teaspoon salt
⅛ teaspoon black pepper
2 cups milk
¾ cup shredded sharp cheddar cheese
8 ounces elbow macaroni, cooked and drained

In medium saucepan, melt butter over medium-low heat. Stir flour into butter until smooth and bubbly. Stir in salt and pepper. Gradually add milk, stirring constantly. Continue to cook and stir until thickened. Add cheese, stirring until melted. Alternate layers of cheese sauce and cooked macaroni in 8x10-inch baking dish. Bake at 350 degrees for 20 minutes or until hot and bubbly.

Ham and Rice Casserole

2 cups cooked rice
2 cups diced cooked ham
1½ cups mixed vegetables, cooked and drained
1 (10½ ounce) can condensed cream of mushroom soup
½ cup milk
½ teaspoon salt
¼ teaspoon pepper
1 cup butter-flavored cracker crumbs

In large bowl, combine rice, ham, vegetables, mushroom soup, milk, salt, and pepper. Spoon mixture into buttered casserole dish and top evenly with cracker crumbs. Bake at 325 degrees for 30 minutes or until hot and bubbly.

Carolina Tuna Casserole

- 4 tablespoons butter
- 3 tablespoons finely chopped onion
- 2 tablespoons finely chopped green bell pepper
- 2 tablespoons flour
- ¾ teaspoon seasoned salt
- ⅛ teaspoon black pepper
- 1 cup milk
- 1 (10 ounce) can condensed cream of mushroom soup
- 8 ounces rigatoni, cooked and drained
- 1 (8 ounce) can tuna, drained
- ½ cup frozen peas, thawed
- 1 cup shredded cheddar cheese, divided
- ¼ cup butter-flavored cracker crumbs

Melt butter in large saucepan. Add chopped onion and green pepper and sauté over low heat until tender. Add flour, salt, and pepper. Cook, stirring constantly, until smooth and bubbly. Add milk and mushroom soup. Stir over low heat until smooth and thickened. Add cooked pasta, tuna, peas, and ½ cup cheese to sauce mixture, stirring constantly. Pour mixture into buttered 2-quart casserole dish. Top with remaining cheese and cracker crumbs. Bake at 350 degrees for 30 to 40

Fettuccini Alfredo

6 ounces fettuccini, uncooked
¼ cup butter or margarine
¾ cup Parmesan cheese, grated
½ cup heavy whipping cream
2 tablespoons fresh parsley, chopped (optional)

Cook fettuccini according to package directions; drain and set aside on serving dish. Meanwhile, in small saucepan, melt butter or margarine over medium heat; gradually stir in cheese, then add whipping cream, stirring until well blended. Continue heating sauce, stirring constantly, just to boiling point. Remove from heat; stir in parsley, if desired. Pour sauce over noodles, and serve. Can also add chicken, shrimp, or bacon bits.

Crescent Roll Chicken

1 (10 ounce) can condensed cream of chicken soup
½ cup cheddar cheese, shredded (optional)
½ cup milk
1 (8 ounce) can refrigerated crescent roll dough
3 boneless, skinless chicken breasts, cooked and cut into small pieces

Combine soup, cheese, and milk. Pour half of mixture into 9x13-inch pan. Separate rolls; place as much cut-up chicken in each roll as will fit; roll up, tucking in edges. Place in pan. Spoon other half of sauce over rolls. Sprinkle shredded cheese over all (optional). Bake at 350 degrees for 25 to 30 minutes or until lightly browned.

Note: Recipe can be doubled by using 29-ounce can of cream of chicken soup; use more cheese and 2 cans of crescent rolls.

Festive Fajitas

3 to 4 boneless, skinless chicken breasts
1 tablespoon vegetable oil
¼ teaspoon garlic powder
1 cup green bell pepper, cut into strips
¾ cup onion, sliced
1 (10 ounce) block Mexican-style processed cheese
1 package 8-inch flour tortillas
1 cup tomato, chopped

Slice chicken breasts into thin strips. In large skillet, stir-fry chicken in oil and garlic powder until no longer pink. Add green pepper strips and onion slices. Continue to stir-fry for 5 minutes. Cut cheese into cubes and add to chicken mixture. Stir until cheese is melted; do not allow to boil. Place desired amount of chicken-cheese mixture in center of each tortilla. Top with chopped tomatoes. Fold.

Mexican Casserole

1 pound ground beef
½ onion, chopped
1 (10 ounce) can condensed cream of chicken soup
8 ounces taco sauce
1 can enchilada sauce
1 package corn tortillas
Cheddar cheese, shredded
1 can sliced ripe black olives (optional)

In large skillet, brown meat and onion; drain. Add soup and sauces, mixing well. In 9x13-inch casserole dish, layer half the tortillas, half the meat mixture, then half the cheese; repeat. Top with olives, if desired. Bake at 350 degrees for 20 to 30 minutes.

Pecan-Chicken Casserole

2 cups cooked chicken, chopped
½ cup pecans, chopped
2 teaspoons minced onion
2 cups celery, chopped
1 cup mayonnaise
2 teaspoons lemon juice
1 cup potato chips, broken
½ cup cheddar cheese, shredded

In large bowl, mix first 6 ingredients together. Place in greased 1½-quart casserole dish. In small bowl, mix chips and cheese and sprinkle on top. Bake uncovered at 350 degrees for 30 minutes.

Oven Beef Stew

    1 pound beef stew meat, cut up
    1 package onion soup mix
    1 can beef broth
    1 (10 ounce) can condensed cream of mushroom soup
    1 soup can of water
    Add desired amounts of the following:
    Carrots, peeled and cut into chunks
    Potatoes, peeled and cut into chunks
    Onions, peeled and cut into chunks.

In Dutch oven or large pot, combine all ingredients; mix well. Cook in oven or in 4- or 6-quart roaster for 3 hours at 300 degrees.

Traditional Cornish Hen

4 (1 pound each) Cornish game hens
Lemon juice
Garlic cloves, crushed
½ teaspoon garlic salt
¼ teaspoon white pepper
½ teaspoon sage
½ teaspoon thyme
½ teaspoon onion powder
1 cup chicken broth

Clean hens with lemon juice and pat dry. Rub skin with crushed garlic cloves. Combine dry seasonings in bowl and season hens inside and out. Place hens in roasting pan; add chicken broth. Cook in preheated 450-degree oven for 15 minutes; reduce heat to 375 degrees, and cook for 30 additional minutes or until juices run clear.

Chicken Diane

4 large boneless chicken breast halves
½ teaspoon salt
½ teaspoon black pepper
2 tablespoons olive oil, divided
2 tablespoons butter or margarine, divided
3 tablespoons chopped fresh chives
Juice of ½ lemon
3 tablespoons chopped fresh parsley
2 teaspoons Dijon mustard
¼ cup chicken broth

Place each chicken breast between two sheets of waxed paper and pound to flatten slightly. Sprinkle chicken with salt and pepper. Set aside. In large skillet, heat 1 tablespoon each of oil and butter or margarine. Cook each chicken breast in skillet for 4 minutes on each side. Transfer to warm serving platter. Add chives, lemon juice, parsley, and mustard to skillet. Cook for 15 seconds, whisking constantly. Whisk in broth and stir until sauce is smooth. Whisk in remaining oil and butter. Pour sauce over chicken and serve immediately. Yield: 4 servings.

May you have the gladness of Christmas which is Hope;
The spirit of Christmas which is Peace;
The heart of Christmas which is Love.

AVA V. HENDRICKS

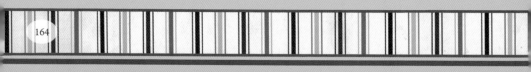

On the tenth day of Christmas
my true love sent to me:

Ten Salads a-Crunching

Christmas Salad Luncheon

Salads are a big favorite with ladies, especially at a time of year when we're all consuming a lot of high-calorie foods and treats—so invite your friends to your home for a Christmas salad luncheon. Plan to serve at least three of the great salad recipes in this section. Choose one that features greens, one with lots of protein, and one that's sweet and fruity. Bake some homemade bread, rolls, or muffins, and serve them warm along with a refreshing herbal iced tea.

Since your salads will probably look busy on the plate, choose solid-colored dishes and plain tall tea glasses if you have them. Use your nicest linens to dress up and make an occasion of a simple meal. A solid tablecloth with contrasting Christmas runners placed perpendicular lengthwise and across the table creates an unusual and interesting look and act as chargers or place mats at each setting.

Create a centerpiece that will complement, not compete, with your table linens. Christmas cactuses are blooming this time of year; place one in a pretty pot amid greenery. Avoid big, showy cut flowers that will go better with a more formal function. As always, keep your centerpiece low, so everyone has a good view of everyone else.

During lunch, you may want to discuss with your friends a few ideas for starting a regular group get-together to begin when January's gloom descends. Book clubs are great and lively fun and meeting once or twice weekly to walk together or exercise to a workout video makes it less of a hassle. Consider a Bible study or simply rotate houses for lunch once a month.

Serve your guests a dessert with a bit more substance like Double-Chocolate Mud Bars or Angel Cake Surprise (see desserts section). When lunch is light and healthy, people won't mind so indulging themselves a bit. Offer a good strong brewed coffee and a pot of hot tea with dessert.

Shop discount outlets for pretty little journal books with blank pages. If you can find them with a Christmas theme, all the better. Write a personal Christmas blessing on the inside front page to each friend in attendance along with the date. Or give small, purse-size tubes of a good hand moisturizer. They are much appreciated this time of year! Tie a ribbon around whatever you choose, and place one at each setting.

Effortless Entertaining Tips:

*Wash lettuce or other salad greens well ahead to dry, cool, and crisp up before you use them. Even greens bought in handy ready-packs will benefit from an ice-cold rinse.

*Certain fat-free gelatins, cream cheeses, and whipped toppings taste as good as the full-calorie varieties. Experiment to find ones you like.

*Keep the theme of your luncheon relaxed and easy with just a bit of flair. Encourage less experienced hostesses by showing that it doesn't take a lot of time or money to put together a simple event.

> *And she brought forth her firstborn son, and wrapped him in swaddling clothes, and laid him in a manger.*
>
> LUKE 2:7 KJV

Champagne Salad

1 (8 ounce) package cream cheese, softened
¾ cup sugar
1 (20 ounce) can crushed pineapple, drained
1 (10 ounce) package frozen strawberries, with juice
2 bananas, sliced
½ cup chopped nuts
1 (16 ounce) container frozen whipped topping, thawed

In mixing bowl, beat cream cheese with sugar; set aside. In separate bowl, fold together pineapple, strawberries with juice, bananas, nuts, and whipped topping. Gently combine with cream cheese mixture. Pour into 9x13-inch dish and freeze completely. To serve, thaw slightly and cut into squares. Keep leftovers frozen. Yield: 12 to 16 servings.

Candy Apple Salad

2 cups water
¼ cup red cinnamon candies
1 (3 ounce) package cherry-flavored gelatin
½ cup chopped celery
1½ cups chopped Granny Smith apples
½ cup chopped walnuts

In saucepan, bring water to boil. Add cinnamon candies, stirring until candies are dissolved. Remove from heat and add gelatin; stir until dissolved. Cool slightly, then refrigerate until gelatin begins to thicken. Add remaining ingredients; blend well. Pour into 8-inch square dish and chill until firm. Yield: 6 servings.

Christmas Crunch Salad

1½ cups broccoli florets
1½ cups cauliflower florets
1 red onion, chopped
2 cups cherry tomatoes, cut in half

Dressing:
1 cup mayonnaise
½ cup sour cream
1 tablespoon vinegar
2 tablespoons sugar
Salt and pepper to taste

Combine vegetables in large bowl. Set aside. In small bowl, whisk together dressing ingredients. Pour over vegetables and gently stir to coat. Chill for at least 2 hours before serving. Yield: 6 servings.

Cranberry Salad

1 (3 ounce) package cherry-flavored gelatin
1 cup hot water
1 can whole-berry cranberry sauce
1 cup sour cream
½ cup chopped pecans

In bowl, mix gelatin with hot water. Stir until dissolved. Refrigerate until slightly congealed. Stir in cranberry sauce, sour cream, and pecans. Pour into gelatin mold and refrigerate until completely set. Yield: 4 to 6 servings.

Layered Broccoli-Cauliflower Salad

6 slices bacon
1 cup broccoli florets
1 cup cauliflower florets
3 hard-boiled eggs, chopped
½ cup chopped red onion
1 cup mayonnaise
½ cup sugar
2 tablespoons white wine vinegar
1 cup shredded cheddar cheese

In large skillet, cook bacon over medium-high heat until crispy. Crumble and set aside. In medium glass salad bowl, layer broccoli, cauliflower, eggs, then onion. Prepare dressing by whisking together in small bowl the mayonnaise, sugar, and vinegar. Drizzle dressing over top of vegetables. Sprinkle crumbled bacon and cheese over dressing. Chill completely to blend flavors. Yield: 8 servings.

Orange Sherbet Salad

2 (3 ounce) packages orange-flavored gelatin
1 cup boiling water
1 cup orange juice
1 pint orange sherbet
1 (11 ounce) can mandarin oranges, drained and cut up
1 (8 ounce) can crushed pineapple, drained
2 bananas, peeled and sliced
1 cup sour cream
1 cup mini marshmallows

In serving dish or bowl, dissolve gelatin in boiling water; add orange juice and sherbet. Stir until sherbet is melted. Add fruit; chill until firm. In small bowl, combine sour cream and marshmallows; spread over top of salad just before

Merry Vegetable Salad

1 (15 ounce) can whole-kernel corn, drained
1 large tomato, seeded and chopped
1 cup frozen peas
½ cup chopped celery
⅓ cup chopped green bell pepper
¼ cup chopped red bell pepper
¼ cup finely chopped onion

Dressing:
¼ cup sour cream
2 tablespoons mayonnaise
2 teaspoons white vinegar
¼ teaspoon salt
⅛ teaspoon black pepper

In large bowl, combine vegetables. In small bowl, whisk together dressing ingredients. Just before serving, add dressing to vegetables and toss to coat. Yield: 6 to 8 servings.

Apple Tree Salad

2 cups apples, chopped
1 cup raisins
⅓ cup pecans or walnuts, chopped
1 cup celery, diced
½ cup mayonnaise
1 tablespoon sugar (optional)
Pinch cinnamon

In large bowl, combine apples, raisins, walnuts, and celery. In small bowl, blend mayonnaise and sugar, if desired. Pour over apple mixture and mix well. Sprinkle cinnamon over top of salad. Serve.

Strawberry-Orange Salad

2 cups boiling water
2 (3 ounce) packages strawberry-flavored gelatin
1 (10 ounce) package frozen strawberries,
    thawed and drained, juice reserved
⅓ cup orange juice
1 (11 ounce) can mandarin oranges, drained
⅓ cup sour cream

In large bowl, pour boiling water over gelatin; stir until gelatin is dissolved. Combine reserved strawberry juice and orange juice in small bowl; stir into gelatin. Reserve 1 tablespoon gelatin-juice mixture; set aside. Cover gelatin mixture and chill until slightly thickened. Gently stir in strawberries and oranges. Pour mixture into gelatin mold. Cover and refrigerate until set. Meanwhile, blend sour cream and reserved 1 tablespoon gelatin mixture in small bowl. Cover; refrigerate until serving time. Serve sour cream topping with salad. Yield: 8 servings.

Strawberry Pretzel Salad

¾ cup butter or margarine, melted
3 tablespoons sugar
2 cups crushed pretzels
1 (8 ounce) package cream cheese, softened
¾ cup sugar
1 (8 ounce) container frozen whipped topping, thawed
2 (3 ounce) packages strawberry-flavored gelatin
2 cups boiling water
1 (16 ounce) package frozen strawberries
1 (8 ounce) can crushed pineapple, drained

In bowl, mix butter or margarine, 3 tablespoons sugar, and crushed pretzels; press mixture into 9x13-inch pan. Bake at 350 degrees for 10 minutes. Cool completely. In mixing bowl, beat cream cheese with ¾ cup sugar. Fold in whipped topping. Spread evenly over cooled pretzel crust. In bowl, combine gelatin with boiling water. Stir to dissolve. Mix in frozen strawberries and pineapple. Allow gelatin to set slightly. Pour gelatin over cream cheese mixture. Refrigerate until completely set. Yield: 12 to 15 servings.

Strawberry Salad

2 (8 ounce) packages cream cheese
2 tablespoons mayonnaise
2 tablespoons sugar
2 (10 ounce) packages frozen strawberries, partially thawed
   and sweetened
2 cups mini marshmallows
1 (12 ounce) can crushed pineapple, drained
3½ cups whipped topping
½ cup chopped walnuts

In large bowl, blend cream cheese, mayonnaise, and sugar. Add remaining ingredients. Pour into festive gelatin mold and freeze thoroughly. Remove salad from freezer 15 to 20 minutes before serving.

Ambrosia

3 (15 ounce) cans fruit cocktail, drained
1 (11 ounce) can mandarin oranges, drained
1 cup mini marshmallows
1 cup sweetened, flaked coconut
2 bananas, sliced
1 jar maraschino cherries, drained and halved
1 (5 ounce) can evaporated milk

Combine all ingredients in large bowl. Refrigerate for at least 1 hour before serving. Yield: 6 servings.

Green Seven-Layer Salad

6 cups chopped lettuce, divided
Salt and pepper to taste
6 hard-boiled eggs, sliced
2 cups frozen peas, thawed
1½ cups bacon, cooked crisp, drained, and crumbled
2 cups shredded cheddar cheese
1 cup mayonnaise
2 tablespoons sugar
¼ cup sliced green onion
Dash paprika

Place 3 cups lettuce in bottom of large bowl and sprinkle with salt and pepper. Layer egg slices over lettuce in bowl and sprinkle with more salt and pepper. Continue with salad layers in this order: peas, remaining lettuce, bacon, and cheese, along with light sprinklings of salt and pepper after each layer. In small bowl, combine mayonnaise and sugar. Spread over top to edge of bowl, covering entire salad. Cover and refriger-ate overnight. Toss before serving. Garnish with green onion and paprika.

Ribbon Salad

2 (3 ounce) packages lime-flavored gelatin
5 cups hot water, divided
4 cups cold water, divided
1 (3 ounce) package lemon-flavored gelatin
8 ounces cream cheese
4 ounces mini marshmallows
½ cup crushed pineapple, drained
1 cup whipped topping
2 (3 ounce) packages cherry-flavored gelatin

In bowl, dissolve lime gelatin in 2 cups hot water; once dissolved, add 2 cups cold water. Pour into 9x13-inch pan and chill until set. In bowl, dissolve lemon gelatin in 1 cup hot water, then add cream cheese and marshmallows. When lemon mixture starts to set, add pineapple and whipped topping. Pour over lime layer and chill until set. In bowl, dissolve cherry gelatin in 2 cups hot water; once dissolved, add 2 cups cold water. Chill until cherry mixture starts to set, then pour over lemon salad layer. Chill salad until firm.

Pink Salad

1 (24 ounce) carton cottage cheese
1 (3 ounce) package strawberry-flavored gelatin
1 (8 ounce) container frozen whipped topping, thawed
½ cup mini marshmallows
½ cup nuts (optional)

In bowl, mix cottage cheese and gelatin. Gently fold in whipped topping and marshmallows. Stir in nuts if desired. Spoon into serving dish and chill until set. Yield: 8 servings.

Marinated Mushroom-Spinach Salad

½ cup oil
¼ cup white wine vinegar
1 small onion, sliced
½ teaspoon basil
1 teaspoon salt
¾ teaspoon fresh-ground black pepper
½ pound mushrooms, washed and sliced thin
1 pound fresh spinach, washed and torn into bite-size pieces

In medium bowl, combine oil, vinegar, onion, basil, salt, and pepper. Add mushrooms. Let stand at room temperature for 2 hours or refrigerate overnight, stirring occasionally. When ready to serve, place spinach in salad bowl; add mushroom-oil mixture and toss well. Serve at once. Yield: 6 servings.

Copper Carrot Pennies

2 pounds carrots, sliced
1 small green bell pepper
1 medium onion
1 (10 ounce) can condensed tomato soup
½ cup vegetable or canola oil
1 cup sugar
¾ cup vinegar
1 teaspoon prepared mustard
1 teaspoon Worcestershire sauce
Salt and pepper to taste

Slice carrots in even disks. Slice green pepper in rings. Slice onion thinly. Boil carrots until crisp-tender. Alternate layers of carrots, green pepper rings, and onion slices in baking dish. In bowl, combine remaining ingredients and beat until smooth. Pour over vegetables. Refrigerate. Serve cold.

Pearl's Cranberry Salad

1 (3 ounce) package cherry-flavored gelatin
1¾ cups hot water
1 cup fresh cranberries
½ orange, with peel
⅓ cup sugar
½ cup crushed pineapple, drained
¼ cup pecans, chopped
1½ cups whipped topping

In large bowl, dissolve gelatin in hot water. Set aside to cool until syrupy. Grind cranberries and orange and pour into medium-size bowl. Add sugar, pineapple, and pecans to cranberry mixture and stir well. Add to gelatin. Chill until firmly set and spread whipped topping on top.

Mandarin Orange Salad

    2 cups boiling water
    1 (6 ounce) package orange-flavored gelatin
    1 pint orange sherbet
    1 (11 ounce) can mandarin oranges, drained
    1 (8½ ounce) can crushed pineapple, undrained

In mixing bowl, pour boiling water over gelatin. Stir until gelatin is dissolved.
Spoon orange sherbet into gelatin and mix until well combined. Fold in remaining
ingredients. Pour into gelatin mold and refrigerate until firm. Yield: 8 servings.

Are you willing to believe that love is the strongest thing in the world—stronger than hate, stronger than evil, stronger than death—and that the blessed life which began in Bethlehem nineteen hundred years ago is the image and brightness of the Eternal Love? Then you can keep Christmas.

HENRY VAN DYKE

On the eleventh day of Christmas
my true love sent to me:

Eleven Sides a-Steaming

Scrambled Dinner

Usually relegated to the back of cookbooks, side dishes can be incorporated into what is called a "Scrambled Dinner." This is a chance for some truly different, stress-relieving silliness during the holidays.

Start by e-viting a few friends for dinner; a group of eight is just right, because dinner will be served in three courses, and your "waiters" need room to maneuver. This is not a dressy affair; encourage casual, comfortable clothes. Assign each couple one of the side dish recipes you plan to serve, enough for each guest to have a small serving. That's all they need to know. The host provides a meat entrée and dessert, but your guests won't have any idea what you're serving or what anyone else is bringing.

As your friends arrive, whisk their side dish away to the warming drawer or oven. Serve warm cider or a cold punch in the living room to keep your guests out of the kitchen where dinner service is being organized.

Decorate your table for a fun, rowdy party. No candles tonight! Guests will need to see their plates easily. Put on some lively music, and seat guests once everyone has arrived. There are no place settings; the only items for each guest are a menu and a pen.

Create the menus by folding heavy computer paper in half like a greeting card. Use any artwork you like, but make sure the menu can be easily read. When opened, the left side of the menu will be a list of every single item for the meal (including eating utensils, each individual dish and beverage), but each will be cleverly disguised under a new name. Mashed potatoes become "Clouds over Bethlehem," and a butter knife is "Herod's Scepter." If your main dish is beef, you might call it "Cattle are Lowing," a napkin is "Swaddling Clothes," and so on—pull out all your creative genius for this! The right side of the menu contains blank lines under the headings of Course I, Course II, Course III, one line for each item they'll be served from the left side of the menu. Have guests fill out all three courses at once, then write their names at the top and turn them in to servers.

You will need help in the kitchen for this event! Ask a few of your church youth group to come dressed in white shirts, black pants, and a tie. They will be filling orders, carrying them in to each diner, and clearing after each course. Forget the good china and use fun holiday paper products and plastic eating utensils for quick cleanup. While guests are "enjoying" their first course, hostess and servers can be readying and warming foods, straightening up in the kitchen, and getting ready for Courses II and III.

The fun really starts when Course I appears: someone gets a vegetable, dessert, and meat, but has only a toothpick to eat it with! Someone else has unwittingly ordered a napkin, a glass of water, and all his silverware for Course I and has to eat his next two courses with his fingers! (Each course is cleared before the next comes out.) In the kitchen, you will have labeled each category of dinnerware, beverage, and food with its disguised name, so your servers can move around the stations and fill one or two orders at a time.

When the meal is over, invite guests to finish off any of the food, drink, and dessert left in the kitchen, this time filling their own plates!

Send guests home with small, inexpensive puzzle books: crosswords, Sudoku, etc., to hone their decoding and problem-solving skills. Roll them up and tie each with a Christmas ribbon.

Effortless Entertaining Tips:

*Have a good-sized trash receptacle conveniently located in the serving area for quick disposal of each finished course.

*Menus should be served back to diners with each course so they can see that they did, indeed, order "Snowy Boughs" (cauliflower florets), "Snow Shovel" (a spoon), "Angel Fingers" (glazed carrots), or "Sweet Memories" (an after-dinner mint).

*Present a "Good Sport Award" to the diner who got the most discombobulated meal!

*After dinner, call the servers into the dining room, thank them, and send them home with leftovers.

Glazed Carrots

1¼ pounds (about 8 medium) fresh carrots
⅓ cup packed brown sugar
2 tablespoons margarine or butter
½ teaspoon salt
½ teaspoon grated orange peel

Cut carrots in sections 2½ inches in length, then into ⅜-inch strips. In saucepan, bring 1 inch salted water to boil. Add carrots, cover, and bring to boil again. Reduce heat and cook 18 to 20 minutes, or until tender; drain. Combine brown sugar, margarine or butter, salt, and orange peel in 10-inch skillet; stir and cook until bubbly. Add carrots and cook over low heat about 5 minutes, or until carrots are glazed and heated through.

Sweet Potato Crunch

3 pounds sweet potatoes
1 stick unsalted butter, melted, divided
½ cup packed brown sugar
¼ cup orange juice
1½ teaspoons cinnamon
¼ teaspoon salt
1½ cups graham cracker crumbs

Place sweet potatoes in pot of boiling water and cook for 35 to 40 minutes, or until tender; drain. When cool, peel. Preheat oven to 400 degrees. Mash sweet potatoes in large bowl; add 4 tablespoons melted butter, brown sugar, orange juice, cinnamon, and salt; mix until smooth. In separate bowl, combine graham cracker crumbs and remaining 4 tablespoons melted butter. Pour sweet potato mixture into greased 9-inch square baking pan and top with crumb mixture. Bake 15 to 20 minutes or until hot and bubbly. Yield: 8 to 10 servings.

Cheddar Corn Casserole with Red and Green Peppers

    1 stick butter, divided
    1 large onion, chopped
    ½ medium green bell pepper, diced
    ½ medium red bell pepper, diced
    1 garlic clove, minced
    3 eggs
    1 cup sour cream
    1 (16 ounce) can cream-style corn
    ⅓ cup yellow cornmeal
    ¼ teaspoon salt
    ¼ teaspoon black pepper
    1¼ cups (5 ounces) shredded cheddar cheese

Preheat oven to 350 degrees. Melt butter in medium-size skillet over medium heat. Add onion and green and red peppers, and cook, stirring occasionally for 3 to 5 minutes or until peppers are soft. Add garlic and cook an additional 1 to 2 minutes; remove from heat and set aside. Melt remaining butter and combine with eggs and sour cream in large bowl and whisk until smooth. Stir in corn, cornmeal, salt, and pepper. Add cheese and cooked pepper mixture. Pour into greased 2-quart casserole and bake for 30 to 35 minutes until puffed, golden, and set in center. Yield: 8 to 10 servings.

Barbecued Beans

1 pound ground beef
1 onion, chopped
4 (1 pound) cans pork and beans
1 tablespoon Worcestershire sauce
Salt and pepper to taste
2 tablespoons vinegar
2 tablespoons brown sugar
½ cup ketchup
1 dash chili powder

Brown ground beef and onion in large skillet; drain off fat. Add remaining ingredients. Transfer to casserole dish and bake at 350 degrees for 35 minutes. Or may be left in skillet to cook over low heat, stirring often, until boiling, then let simmer for 10 to 15 minutes.

Creamy Corn

1 (20 ounce) package frozen corn
1 (8 ounce) package cream cheese, softened
½ cup butter
3 teaspoons sugar
6 tablespoons water

Place corn, cream cheese, butter, sugar, and water in slow cooker. Cook on low for 4 to 5 hours.

Broccoli and Rice Casserole

3 stalks fresh or 1 box frozen broccoli, steamed
1 cup short- or long-grain brown or white rice, cooked
1 (10 ounce) can condensed cream of chicken soup (or cream of celery or
    mushroom soup)
½ cup mayonnaise
3 cups cheddar, Colby, or other favorite cheese, shredded, divided
Salt and pepper to taste

In large bowl, mix steamed broccoli, cooked rice, soup, mayonnaise, and 1 cup cheese together. Add salt and pepper to taste. Pour into casserole dish, and top with remaining cheese. Bake at 375 degrees for 20 to 30 minutes or until cheese on top is bubbly.

Tangy Ranch Green Beans

2 tablespoons butter or margarine
2 packages frozen French-cut green beans, partially thawed
1 can sliced mushrooms, drained
1 envelope ranch dressing mix
3 to 4 slices bacon, cooked and crumbled

In skillet, melt butter or margarine. Stir in green beans and cook until tender. Mix in mushrooms and ranch dressing mix. Heat through. Before serving, sprinkle crumbled bacon over beans.

Carrots in Gravy

3 tablespoons butter
2 pounds carrots, peeled and sliced ½-inch thick
1 medium onion, chopped
2 tablespoons flour
1 tablespoon minced parsley
1 cup unsalted chicken stock
½ teaspoon salt
¼ teaspoon black pepper
¼ teaspoon grated nutmeg

Melt butter in large, heavy saucepan over low heat. Add carrots, cover, and cook, stirring occasionally for 20 to 25 minutes, until firm-tender. Using slotted spoon, place carrots in bowl; set aside. Add onion to butter remaining in saucepan. Increase heat to medium and cook until lightly browned. Sprinkle in flour and cook, stirring constantly, until flour is golden. Add parsley and whisk in stock. Bring to boil, continuing to whisk until gravy is smooth and thick. Season with salt, pepper, and nutmeg. Return carrots to saucepan and reduce heat to low, cooking until heated through. Serve hot.

Almond Rice

1¾ cups water
½ cup orange juice
½ teaspoon salt
1 cup uncooked long-grain rice
2 tablespoons butter or margarine
2 tablespoons brown sugar
½ cup sliced natural almonds
1 teaspoon minced crystallized ginger
¼ teaspoon grated orange peel
Additional orange peel (optional)

In medium saucepan, bring water, orange juice, and salt to boil; gradually add rice, stirring constantly. Cover, reduce heat, and simmer for 20 to 25 minutes or until rice is tender and liquid is absorbed. Meanwhile, melt butter or margarine and brown sugar in small skillet over medium heat. Stir in almonds and ginger; sauté for 2 minutes or until almonds are lightly browned. When rice is done, add almond mixture and grated orange peel to rice; stir gently to combine. Garnish with additional orange peel if desired. Yield: 4 servings.

Amish Dressing

8 tablespoons butter, divided
1 loaf stale bread, cubed
½ cup carrots, shredded
1 cup celery, finely chopped
¼ cup onion, finely chopped
6 eggs, well beaten
2 cups milk
1 cup boiled potatoes, chopped
2 cups chicken broth with shredded chicken
2 teaspoons chicken boullion
Salt and pepper

Melt 4 tablespoons butter in large frying pan; toss bread in butter until toasted. Set aside. In frying pan, melt remaining 4 tablespoons butter and sauté carrots, celery, and onion until tender. Combine toasted bread, sautéed vegetables, eggs, milk, potatoes, broth, and soup base. Season to taste with salt and pepper. Pour into baking pan and bake at 325 degrees for 45 minutes.

Noodles

3 eggs
3 cups flour, plus flour for dusting
3 teaspoons salt
¾ cup milk
3 teaspoons baking powder

In large bowl, mix all ingredients together and shape dough into ball. If mixture is sticky, add more flour. If too dry to form ball shape, add more milk. Once in ball, knead with hands. Spread flour on flat surface and flatten ball of dough with heel of hand, then roll with rolling pin to desired thickness. Sprinkle flour on dough; turn dough over to flour other side. Use pizza cutter to cut noodles to desired width. Coat noodles with more flour and allow to air dry for 4 to 6 hours. Shake off excess flour. Store in paper bag for couple of days or freeze in plastic bag. To use, cook in boiling water or broth for 10 minutes (approximately 20 if frozen).

Creamy Mashed Potatoes

3 pounds potatoes, peeled and quartered
1½ sticks butter
6 ounces cream cheese, softened
1 cup shredded cheddar cheese, divided
1 small green bell pepper, finely chopped
6 green onions, finely chopped
½ cup grated Parmesan cheese
¼ cup milk
1 teaspoon salt

In large pot, cover potatoes with water and boil for 15 minutes or until tender; drain and mash. Add butter and cream cheese; beat with electric mixer at medium speed until smooth. Stir in ½ cup cheddar cheese, green pepper, onions, Parmesan cheese, milk, and salt. Spoon into lightly buttered 7x11-inch baking dish. Bake at 350 degrees for 30 to 40 minutes or until thoroughly heated. Sprinkle with remaining cheese; bake for an additional 5 minutes or until cheese melts.

Sloppy Potatoes

3 medium potatoes, sliced
1 medium onion, sliced
1 tablespoon butter
½ teaspoon salt

In medium saucepan, bring all ingredients to boil. Reduce heat to low and cook 15 minutes, stirring occasionally.

Amazing Cauliflower

1 head cauliflower
1 large green bell pepper, chopped
1 large onion, chopped
1 teaspoon salt
3 tablespoons butter
3 tablespoons flour
1½ cups milk
1 cup shredded cheddar cheese, divided
½ cup butter-flavored cracker crumbs

Trim cauliflower into flowerets. Combine cauliflower with green pepper and onion in large saucepan. Cover with water and add salt. Bring to boil. Cover and cook for 10 minutes or until tender. Drain and set aside. In separate saucepan, melt butter over medium-low heat. Stir in flour until smooth and bubbly. Gradually add milk, stirring constantly. Continue cooking and stirring until thickened. Stir in ½ cup cheese. Pour sauce over cauliflower and stir gently. Transfer cauliflower mixture to lightly buttered 1½-quart baking dish. Top with cracker crumbs. Bake at 350 degrees for 30 minutes. Sprinkle with remaining cheese and bake an additional 5 minutes or until cheese melts.

Creamy Corn Casserole

 3 tablespoons butter or margarine, divided
 1 cup finely chopped celery
 ¼ cup finely chopped onion
 ¼ cup finely chopped red bell pepper
 1 (10 ounce) can condensed cream of chicken soup
 3 cups fresh, frozen, or canned corn, drained
 1 (8 ounce) can sliced water chestnuts, drained
 ½ cup soft bread crumbs

Melt 2 tablespoons butter or margarine in medium skillet. Add celery, onion, and red pepper; sauté until vegetables are tender, about 2 minutes. Remove from heat and stir in soup, corn, and water chestnuts. Spoon into greased 2-quart casserole dish. Melt remaining 1 tablespoon butter and toss with bread crumbs. Sprinkle on top of casserole and bake uncovered at 350 degrees for 25 to 30 minutes. Yield: 8 servings.

Green Peas with Celery and Onion

 2 (10 ounce) packages frozen peas
 ½ cup celery, sliced
 1 small onion, thinly sliced
 3 tablespoons margarine or butter, softened
 ¼ teaspoon salt

Cook celery, onion, and peas according to directions on frozen peas package; drain. Stir in margarine or butter and salt.

Roman Pasta Salad

1 pound thin spaghetti (or other pasta)
2 large tomatoes
1 large onion
1 large cucumber
1 large green bell pepper
16 ounces Italian dressing
1 envelope Italian dressing mix

In pot, cook pasta; drain and let cool. Set aside. Dice vegetables. In large bowl, mix vegetables with Italian dressing and mix. Add cooled pasta; refrigerate overnight.

English Pea Casserole

¼ cup butter or margarine
½ cup chopped onion
1 small red bell pepper, chopped
1 (5 ounce) package medium egg noodles
1 (8 ounce) package cream cheese, softened
2 cups (8 ounces) shredded sharp cheddar cheese
1 (10 ounce) package frozen English peas, thawed and drained
1 (2½ ounce) jar mushroom stems and pieces, undrained
½ teaspoon black pepper
10 butter-flavored crackers, crushed

In small skillet, melt butter and sauté onion and red pepper until tender. Set aside. In large pot, cook noodles according to package directions; drain. Add cream cheese and cheddar cheese to hot noodles; stir until cheeses melt. Stir in onion mixture, peas, mushrooms, and pepper. Spoon into greased baking dish and top with cracker crumbs. Cover and bake at 325 degrees for 25 to 30 minutes.

Rebecca's Cornbread Dressing

1 medium onion, chopped
3 stalks celery, chopped
1 green bell pepper, chopped
2 tablespoons butter
1 (8 ounce) package dry cornbread stuffing
1 (8 ounce) package dry herb stuffing
½ cup buttered cracker crumbs
2 eggs
3½ cups chicken broth
Salt and pepper to taste
1½ teaspoons sage

Preheat oven to 350 degrees. In skillet, sauté onion, celery, and green pepper in butter until soft but not brown. In large mixing bowl, combine cooked vegetables, both dry stuffing packages, and cracker crumbs. Stir in eggs and chicken broth. Add salt and pepper to taste. Add sage. Mix well. Spoon into greased 9x13-inch glass baking dish. Bake for 20 minutes or until set and lightly browned.

Christmas may be a day of feasting, or of prayer, but always it will be a day of remembrance—a day in which we think of everything we have ever loved.

Augusta E. Rundel

On the twelfth day of Christmas
my true love sent to me:

Twelve Soups a-Simmering

Casual Soup Buffet

There's nothing quite as satisfying as a hot bowl of soup on a cold winter night! Invite two or three couples over for a casual soup buffet and an evening of fellowship. Encourage them to dress in comfortable clothes for lounging. Assign each couple one of the yummy soup recipes in this section, or one of their own choosing if they have a specialty. Make sure that at least one of the recipes is meat-based.

Have your guests bring their soups in slow cookers. These can be set up around the kitchen for uncrowded service. From a central area like an island, serve warm bread or rolls, a selection of crackers and cheese, sliced fruit, and a dessert.

Hot soup needs a hefty, sturdy bowl, so avoid using plastic or paper if at all possible. Stack matching sets of bowls and a container full of spoons beside each clow cooker. You'll need lots of bowls for this type of event, even if that means borrowing a few sets for the evening. You won't want guests trying to wash their dishes in order to try another kind of soup. Suggest that they stack their dirty bowls by the sink and start fresh.

Use cloth napkins if you have them, but the paper variety is fine, too, as long as they're large and dense—they'll get a lot of use.

Make decaffeinated coffee just ahead of guests' arrival. Use a pump pot to keep it hot and ready near the dessert. Have dessert and coffee dishes set up in advance, and don't forget the cream, sugar, and stirring spoons.

Invite your friends to carry their food in around the fire. Use coffee table, end tables, or raised hearth as eating surfaces. Gather up lots of throw pillows for those who like sitting on the floor. Make a few serving trays available for those using their laps. You want to be sure everyone is comfortable and has a place to sit, so you may have to bring in a few more chairs or an extra coffee table ahead of time.

Choose a weekend night for this gathering so your friends will feel free to linger late. The mood overall should be super casual, intimate, and no-fuss. This is an evening for you to hang out with friends. You have no table to set, no centerpiece to create, no puttering in the kitchen, no waiting on guests.

A fire in the fireplace and strategically placed candles will create a warm and comfortable atmosphere, and your Christmas decorations should be all you need. Add a lovely poinsettia if you like. They are especially beautiful in a room bathed in candlelight.

If your guests sense you are relaxed and enjoying yourself, they will relax as well. Put on some serene, low-volume Christmas music and settle in, chill out, and chat. The holidays really are the best time of the year.

Effortless Entertaining Tips:

*Make sure you set up each slow cooker near an outlet; have extra extension cords available in case you need them, but avoid stretching them across high-traffic areas.

*Turn one side of your kitchen sink into a handy beverage service area. Fill it with ice, and bury your beverages in it. As always, have a large pitcher of ice water available.

*See that your driveway and walk areas are clear of snow and ice.

{
Come to Bethlehem and see Christ whose birth the angels sing;
Come adore on bended knee, Christ the Lord, the newborn King.
Gloria, in excelsis Deo!
Gloria, in excelsis Deo!

TRADITIONAL FRENCH CAROL
}

Broccoli Soup

1 (10 ounce) package frozen broccoli
1 medium onion
1 stick butter
1 (10 ounce) can condensed cream of chicken soup
1 (10 ounce) can condensed cream of celery soup
3 cups milk
1 (6 ounce) block Mexican-style or plain processed cheese
Dash Tabasco

Cook broccoli according to package directions; drain. In large saucepan, sauté onion in butter. Stir in soups and milk. Add cheese and stir until cheese melts. Add broccoli and Tabasco. Heat soup through, but do not boil!

Turkey Bone Soup

Bones and trimmings from one roasted turkey
6 cups water
3 teaspoons chicken bouillon
1½ teaspoons salt
¼ teaspoon ground sage
1 bay leaf
3 medium carrots, sliced
2 stalks celery, sliced
2 medium onions, chopped
½ cup rice or 1 cup dried noodles
2 tablespoons parsley

In large pot, put turkey bones and trimmings in water and add bouillon, salt, sage, and bay leaf. Cover and simmer for 1½ hours. Remove bones. Add carrots, celery, onions, and rice or noodles. Cover and simmer for 30 minutes. Serve garnished with parsley. Yield: 6 to 8 servings.

Peanut Butter Soup

1 cup peanut butter
3 cups milk, divided
½ cup celery, chopped
1½ cups water
1 potato, grated
2 teaspoons salt
½ teaspoon black pepper

In bowl, mix peanut butter with 1 cup milk; heat 2 cups milk in double boiler. In large saucepan, cook celery in water until tender. Add grated potato to celery and cook, stirring mixture until thickened. Add hot milk to cooked vegetables, then blend in peanut butter mixture, salt, and pepper. Beat with mixer to cream soup. Serve hot.

Cheeseburger Soup

8 large potatoes, peeled and chopped
1 small onion, chopped (optional)
1 stalk celery, chopped (optional)
1½ to 2 pounds ground chuck
Salt and pepper to taste
1 (10 ounce) can condensed cheddar cheese soup
2 cups milk
4 tablespoons margarine
1 can cheese sauce

In large pot, boil potatoes and onion and celery, if using, for 15 minutes; drain. In skillet, brown meat, salt, and pepper; drain. Mix with hot potatoes. Add soup, milk, margarine, and cheese sauce and combine ingredients well. Bring to simmer until potatoes are soft.

Cheesy Vegetable Soup

1 quart water
4 cubes chicken bouillon
1 medium onion
1 cup celery, chopped
2½ cups cubed, skinned potatoes
1 (20 ounce) bag frozen mixed vegetables
2 (10 ounce) cans condensed cream of chicken soup
1 (1 pound) block processed cheese, cut up

In large pot, boil water, bouillon cubes, onion, and celery for 20 minutes. Add potatoes and vegetables. Cook for about 1 hour, until potatoes are tender. Add soup and cheese. Stir until cheese is melted. Yield: 8 to 10 servings.

Cream of Wild Rice Soup

1 large onion, chopped
1 large carrot, shredded
1 stalk celery, chopped
¼ cup butter or margarine
½ cup flour
8 cups chicken broth
3 cups cooked wild rice
1 cup cubed, cooked chicken breast
¼ teaspoon salt
¼ teaspoon pepper
1 cup fat-free evaporated milk
¼ cup snipped chives

In large saucepan, sauté onion, carrot, and celery in butter or margarine until tender. Stir in flour, blending well. Gradually add broth. Stir in rice, chicken, salt, and pepper. Bring to boil over medium heat; cook and stir for 2 minutes or until thickened. Stir in milk; cook 3 to 5 minutes to heat through. Garnish servings with chives. Yield: 10 servings (2½ quarts)

Note: For a quick shortcut, use Uncle Ben's wild rice and prepare according to

Tomato Soup

1 (46 ounce) can tomato juice
1 (8 ounce) can tomato sauce
½ cup water
1 tablespoon beef bouillon granules
1 sprig celery leaves, chopped
Half an onion, thinly sliced
½ teaspoon dried basil
2 tablespoons sugar
1 bay leaf
½ teaspoon whole cloves

Combine all ingredients in greased slow cooker. Stir well. Cover. Cook on low 5 to 8 hours. Remove bay leaf and cloves before serving. If you prefer a thicker soup, add ¼ cup instant potato flakes. Stir well and cook 5 minutes longer.

Chicken Chowder

1 cube chicken bouillon
2 cups boiling water
2 cups diced potatoes
½ cup carrots, sliced
½ cup celery, chopped
¼ cup onion, chopped
1½ teaspoons salt
¼ teaspoon black pepper
¼ cup margarine
¼ cup flour
2 cups milk
2 cups (8 ounces) cheddar cheese, shredded
1 cup diced, cooked chicken

In large pot, dissolve bouillon cube in water; add vegetables, salt, and pepper. Cover; simmer 10 minutes. Do not drain; set aside. In large skillet, melt margarine over low heat. Add flour, stirring until bubbly. Slowly add milk and stir until sauce is thickened. Add cheese; stir until melted. Add chicken and undrained vegetables to sauce. Heat through, but do not allow to boil. Yield: 6 to 8 servings.

Salsa Soup

3 cups (26 ounces) corn and black bean mild salsa
6 cups beef broth
¼ cup long-grain white rice, uncooked

Combine all ingredients in slow cooker. Cover. Cook on low 4 to 6 hours, or until rice is tender. Yield: 6 servings.

Mexican Black Bean Soup

1½ boneless chicken breasts, diced
1 envelope low-sodium taco seasoning (dry)
1 (32 ounce) can tomato juice
1 (16 ounce) jar picante salsa
1 bag frozen corn
1 can black beans, drained and rinsed

In large skillet, brown chicken breast pieces in oil. Add ½ cup water and taco seasoning. Simmer for 15 to 30 minutes. Stir in juice and salsa and pour into slow cooker or cook on low in stockpot on stove. Before serving, add corn and black beans. Heat through. May serve with dollop of sour cream and sprinkle of shredded cheddar cheese and cilantro on top.

White Chili

½ cup chopped onion
1 tablespoon oil
1 to 2 cloves minced garlic
1 (4 ounce) can chopped green chilies
2 (19 ounce) cans cannellini beans, drained
1 large can chicken broth
4 cups chopped, cooked chicken breasts
2 teaspoons cumin
1½ teaspoons oregano
½ teaspoon salt
1½ cups grated Monterey Jack cheese

In large skillet, sauté onion and garlic in oil. Add all other ingredients except cheese. Cook all together. Stir in cheese just before serving. Serve with sour cream or salsa if desired.

Old-Fashioned Bean Soup

1 pound dry navy beans, or dry green split peas
1 pound meaty ham bone, or 1 pound ham pieces
1 to 2 teaspoons salt
¼ teaspoon black pepper
½ cup chopped celery leaves
2 quarts water
1 medium onion, chopped
1 bay leaf (optional)

Soak beans or peas overnight. Drain, discarding soaking water. Combine all ingredients in slow cooker. Cover. Cook on high 8 to 9 hours. Remove and debone ham bone, if using; cut meat into bite-size pieces, and stir back into soup. Remove bay leaf before serving.

Cheese Cauliflower Soup

4 cups (1 small head) cauliflower pieces
2 cups water
1 (8 ounce) package cream cheese, cubed
5 ounces American cheese spread
¼ pound dried beef, torn into strips or shredded
½ cup potato flakes or buds

Combine cauliflower and water in saucepan. Bring to boil and cook until tender. Do not drain; set aside. Heat slow cooker on low. Add cream cheese and cheese spread. Pour in cauliflower and water. Gently stir until cheese is dissolved and mixed through cauliflower. Add dried beef and potato flakes. Mix well. Cover. Cook on low 2 to 3 hours.

Broccoli-Mushroom Chowder

1 pound fresh broccoli
8 ounces fresh mushrooms
2 sticks butter
1 cup flour
1 quart chicken stock
1 quart half and half
1 teaspoon garlic salt
¼ teaspoon white pepper
¼ teaspoon crushed tarragon leaves
1 block processed cheese
Fine noodles (cooked)

Clean and cut broccoli into ½-inch pieces. In pot, steam broccoli in ½ cup water until tender. Do not drain. Set aside. Clean and slice mushrooms; set aside. Melt butter in large saucepan over medium heat. Add flour to make roux. Cook for 2 to 4 minutes. Slowly add chicken stock, stirring with wire whisk. Bring to boil. Turn heat to low. Add broccoli, mushrooms, half and half, salt, pepper, tarragon, cheese, and cooked noodles. Heat through, but do not boil.

Macaroni and Cheese Soup

¼ cup margarine
½ cup finely chopped carrots
½ cup finely chopped celery
1 small onion, finely chopped
4 cups milk
1½ cups (6 ounces) shredded
   American cheese
2 tablespoons chicken bouillon

½ teaspoon black pepper
2 tablespoons cornstarch
2 tablespoons water
1 cup elbow macaroni, cooked
1 (8 ounce) can whole-kernel
   corn, drained
½ cup frozen peas

Melt margarine in large skillet. Cook carrots, celery, and onion until tender. Set aside. In saucepan, combine milk and cheese and cook over medium heat until cheese melts, stirring frequently. Stir in bouillon and pepper. In small bowl, combine cornstarch and water, stirring well. Blend into milk mixture. Cook over medium heat, stirring constantly, until mixture thickens and comes to boil. Boil 1 minute, stirring constantly. Stir in macaroni, vegetable mixture, corn, and peas. Cook over low heat until warmed through. Yield: 8 cups.

Onion Soup

4 tablespoons butter
5 cups thinly sliced onions
1 tablespoon flour
Salt to taste
French or garlic bread, sliced and toasted
Cheddar cheese, grated

Melt butter in large pot. Add onions, and cook, stirring often. Stir in flour and cook for 3 minutes. Add salt. Slowly stir in 4 cups water and simmer partially covered for 30 minutes. Serve over slice of French or garlic bread. Top with grated cheddar cheese.

French Onion Soup

    4 large onions, thinly sliced
    ¼ cup butter
    1 tablespoon flour
    4 to 6 cubes beef bouillon
    4 cups water
    1 teaspoon Worcestershire sauce
    3 slices bread, toasted and cut into cubes
    ½ to ¾ pound grated cheese (Gruyère, Monterey Jack, Muenster,
        mozzarella, etc.)
    Parmesan cheese for sprinkling

In large skillet, sauté onions in butter until golden. Stir in flour. Add bouillon, water, and Worcestershire. Simmer 15 to 20 minutes. To serve: ladle soup into bowls, add toasted bread cubes, top with grated cheese. Sprinkle on Parmesan cheese, and brown under broiler.

Corn Chowder

8 slices bacon
3 to 4 tablespoons flour
4 cups milk
4 cups peeled, chopped potatoes
2 (11 ounce) cans whole-kernel corn
2 (11 ounce) cans cream-style corn
4 cups chicken broth

In skillet, fry bacon; reserve grease. Crumble bacon and set aside. In large sauce-pan, combine 3 to 4 teaspoons grease with flour. Boil 1 minute. Slowly add milk. Bring to boil while stirring for 2 minutes. Add potatoes, both cans of corn, broth, and reserved bacon. Sugar may be added to taste.

Our Favorite Chili

1 pound ground beef, browned
   and drained
½ cup chopped onion
½ cup chopped celery
1 clove garlic, crushed
2 to 3 bay leaves
½ teaspoon salt
⅛ teaspoon ground cloves
1 (15 ounce) can spicy chili
   beans

1½ cups whole tomatoes
   (home canned, if possible)
1 tablespoon chili powder
1 to 2 tablespoons brown sugar
1 cup water

Garnish:
Chopped onion
Grated cheddar or Colby-Jack
   cheese

After browning and draining meat, add onion, celery, and garlic to skillet. Cook until onion is tender. Add remaining ingredients and simmer for ½ to 1 hour to blend flavors. Discard bay leaves. Garnish with onions and cheese just before serving.

INDEX

BREADS

BREAKFAST DISHES

CANDIES

COOKIES

DESSERTS